Financial Intelligence for New Entrepreneurs

Ultimate Guidebook to Help Improve Your Money Thinking and Mental Wealth to Be Ready for Challenging Business Circumstances

Bourke T. Johnsen

Table of Contents

Introduction

In our world today, we are bombarded with success stories of various entrepreneurs who started from nothing but are now easily making millions. How did they get there? What did they do that's different from the rest of us? Although there is no clear cut answer to this, there has been significant research that has shown that successful entrepreneurs have a different mindset, skills, and habits than others.

A successful entrepreneur is a person that is made of financial intelligence, a strong mindset, healthy habits, and self-discipline. In fact, the mindset and habits make up at least 50% of a successful entrepreneur. Simply having financial intelligence or financial skills does not make a person a successful entrepreneur. In reality, a person with the right mindset and habits but without ANY financial intelligence will have a higher chance of success than a person without mindset but with financial intelligence. Financial intelligence can be easily learned by reading books or going to school, but a person's discipline and mindset have to be something that is constantly practiced.

Entrepreneurs are different from so many other careers, as there is literally nobody to hold you accountable. In most jobs, you may have a manager, boss, or partner that will follow up with you on how your work is going or if you are achieving your targets and goals. With entrepreneurship, you are the sole person that is responsible for all the business duties and the managerial aspects. You are acting as the frontline worker AND executive at the same time. Obviously, when you have enough success, you can definitely hire help, but until then, you are responsible for everything starting from tedious tasks like filing all the way to business strategy. This is why learning the right mindset and habits is crucial as, without it, it is easy to become lost and distracted.

Keep in mind that choosing your line of business as an entrepreneur is important as well. For instance, if your dream is to start your own brewery, you must have some knowledge of beer and beverage production. If not, it is still possible to achieve this goal, but you need to invest more time into learning these skills from scratch. Choosing the business you want to create has to be strategic- based on your existing skills and background. It is okay to choose something that you have no experience in, but you have to be prepared to commit the time and energy into a steeper learning curve. For instance, if you have experience in landscaping, then starting your own landscaping business or renovations business may be the most strategic move for you. On the other hand, choosing to start your own restaurant may not be the best move for you, considering you don't have any existing skills.

Moreover, entrepreneurs commonly get stuck on the same mistake, funding. Many entrepreneurs will spend most of their time trying to find funding rather than rethinking their business or building a different plan if they are unable to find enough investors. If you want to be successful, you cannot simply just have one plan where if one step fails, your whole plan will go out the window. Instead, you need to have various backup plans based on the cards you are dealt. Giving up is extremely common in the world of entrepreneurship, and you have probably heard of various instances where people have given up on their business simply due to some failures. Successful entrepreneurs are people that have been faced with failure and have come up with various backup plans to fix it. The only way to ensure that you will be able to bounce back from failure is to build the right mindsets and habits. No amount of financial training or financial intelligence will help you overcome something like that. This book will teach you various methods to help you overcome tough situations like failure.

Throughout this book, I will be teaching you about all the skills you will require to become a successful entrepreneur. In the first half of the book, I will be teaching you how to develop the right mindset, habits, and productivity that you will require to achieve success. In the second half of the book, I will be covering various financial strategies that you may find helpful for your business. These two parts of the book work hand in hand to ensure you are a well-rounded entrepreneur who has both the mindset and the financial skills to build a successful business. It's completely okay if you are just starting out in your career, and you lack the financial background. As I mentioned, your mindset and habits are almost more important than those financial skills. Financial skills can be learned easily with a little bit of studying, but things like mindset, habit, and perseverance are skills that you need to practice often.

In the first half of this book, I will teach you about financial intelligence and the characteristics of a financially intelligent person. Then, we will move on to the topic of mindset. In that chapter, I will teach you about the four characteristics of a financially intelligent and successful entrepreneur mindset. This includes learning about self-discipline, healthy habits, low procrastination, and skill improvement. We will also learn about the growth mindset and how to lose your fixed mindset. After that, we will begin learning about the topic of self-discipline. I will teach you what self-discipline actually is, where it comes from, and areas that you can improve to help yourself become more self-disciplined. In the next chapter, I will provide you with a step by step guide on how you can achieve self-discipline by implementing a few different things into your life. Next, we will touch upon the topic of habits. I will teach you about how habits are formed and how you can use that knowledge to implement habits that all successful entrepreneurs have. This is crucial as learning the right habits will make accomplishing tasks easier and smoother. Once you have an idea of the habits that you need to build, I will then teach you about a couple of strategies that will help you with your skill improvement. As entrepreneurs, you probably already know that you need to keep improving and learning your skills to stay ahead of the game. Becoming stagnant isn't an option, and if you do, you will get beat out by a competitor. In that chapter, I will teach you about two strategies that will help you learn skills faster and to help you accomplish more goals. Once we are finished with that, we will cover the topic of procrastination. This is one of the biggest obstacles that entrepreneurs face as they don't have anyone to hold them accountable. At this point in the book, we will move on to learning about financial skills. In the second half of this book, I will start by teaching you about the competencies of a money manager and other basic skills such as how to read/analyze income statements, balance sheets, and cash flows. After that, we will spend some time on the financial must-knows for entrepreneurs, and I will teach you about terms like ROIs, margins, break-evens, and fixed/variable costs. I will also walk you through the calculations of these numbers to ensure that you are doing those properly for your own financials. Once we've covered that, we will move onto studying more about sales and expenses. We will spend some time learning about strategies we can use to increase sales, distribution channels, and many more. Towards the end of the book, I will spend a chapter teaching you about financial management. I will cover topics on bad financial decisions you should avoid, and I will walk you through various types of accounting methods to help you produce better results. In the last couple of chapters, I will round things up by providing you with more tips to help you become successful in your business. I will spend a little bit more time teaching you about failures and how you can accept them and grow with them, not be defined by them.

So without further ado, let's dive right into our many topics. We have got a lot to cover, so keep yourself open-minded and ready to learn.

Chapter 1: What Is Financial Intelligence?

Financial intelligence is something that everyone has deep inside of them; however, not many people know how to use it to their full potential. Some people have more awareness of financial intelligence and are naturally better at using their money to create more money. Being financially intelligent does not mean that you have to work yourself to the bone; it simply means that you need to have a certain set of skills to help you work smartly. These skills are generally in the form of self-discipline, mindset, and good habits.

The more you understand what financial intelligence is, the easier it will be for you to understand how to work with your money. In most cases, successful self-made people are always those with high financial intelligence. So let's first define financial intelligence. Financial intelligence is the ability to understand the ins and outs of various financial situations; this can vary from your company's finances, the finances of the company you work for, or your own personal finances. In this chapter, you will learn the ways that financial intelligence can apply to you and some characteristics of a financially intelligent person.

Aspects of Financial Intelligence

In this subchapter, I will teach you about some aspects that financial intelligence will help you with, including some characteristics of financially intelligent people.

1. Financial intelligence can help you increase your wealth

Everybody wants to increase their wealth, that is a common fact. Those with high financial intelligence are simply more natural at doing it. Regardless of whether you are an entrepreneur or not, managing your money is important. People make a lot of money out of their existing money simply because they can control their cash flow at all times. You don't have to own a business to be financially intelligent, keeping track of your personal expenses, and managing that is enough to grow your financial intelligence.

2. Financial intelligence changes the way you relate to money

As we mentioned earlier, your mindset is crucial to your entrepreneurial success. However, your mindset is also very important and has a large effect on your financial intelligence and your success at it. Successful money people control their money, and they don't let their money control them. They decide where the money goes and doesn't allow money to determine where they go. Financially intelligent people are not afraid of money; they usually have complete control over all their finances.

3. Financially intelligent people have knowledge about money

There is a big difference between what you know about money and what your beliefs are about money. For most people, they only understand the purchasing power than money brings, and that's about it. However, financially intelligent people know more than just that. They understand what their assets are and what their liabilities are. They understand the difference between a debit and credit card, and usually, it's the lack of knowledge that causes people to make financial mistakes leading them to be in huge debt.

4. Financially intelligent people know what to do with their money

Most people think that they aren't making enough money, although this is true in some cases, many people are not utilizing their money correctly. When you aren't utilizing your money correctly, people often believe that they are not making enough. The caveat to this is that the more money a person makes, the more they are inclined to spend. Financially intelligent people are not constantly chasing after more people; they typically find success by controlling what they spend their earnings on. Typically, a financially intelligent person would aim to save at least 10% of their income, and they never ever touch it. That 10% is saved for investment purposes or kept as emergency money.

5. Financially intelligent people have both short and long term goals

When it comes to money goals, financially intelligent people usually have a set of short term and long term goals. The ability to differentiate between these two types of goals will keep you balanced and focused. People typically forget about their long-term goals when they are faced with the simplicity of achieving their short term goals. To build future wealth, you MUST focus on your long term goals just as much as you focus on your short term goals. Typically, short term goals would be saving up for a 2-week vacation, while long-term goals would be saving up for a mortgage or business investment. If you spend the first $2,000 you save on a vacation, none of that money will ever touch your long-term goals. Financially intelligent people make sure to always be achieving both without losing sight of either.

Self-Discipline Is The Key To Financial Success

Mindset is crucial when it comes to financial intelligence. The way you think and feel about money has everything to do with how you spend it and save it. People with negative mindsets towards money such as; "I never have enough of it anyway, might as well buy this new television now" or "If I don't spend it on something I like, the money will go elsewhere." Mindsets like this cause your finances to always be in shortage and will get you stuck in a vicious cycle. Financially intelligent people typically have strong self-discipline. In many cases, self-discipline is the key to financial success.

Many researchers suggest that the single most important thing in a person's ability to become financially successful is their level of self-discipline. Self-discipline is responsible for helping people stay focused on reaching their goals, gives them the grit that they need to stick with difficult tasks, and allows them to overcome barriers and discomforts as they push yourself to achieve greater things. Let's refresh our memory on the definition of self-discipline. Self-discipline is the ability of a person to control their impulses, reactions, behaviors, and emotions. It allows them to let go of instant gratification in exchange for long-term gain and satisfaction. It's the act of saying no when you really want to say yes. Self-discipline isn't about living a restrictive and boring life without any enjoyment. In fact, it's almost impossible to be 100% self-disciplined in every single area of your life. Rather than trying to be disciplined at everything you do, you can use it to focus on the things that are most important to you. In this chapter, we will be discussing all the reasons why self-discipline is crucial to a person's financial success. We will be going through multiple reasons as to why this is true, and I will provide you with a few tips that will help increase your self-discipline overall.

1. People cannot achieve their financial goals without using self-discipline.

People cannot achieve their financial goals without self-discipline, so make sure you are supplementing your goals with a self-discipline list. It will help you focus on the tasks and behaviors that you need to perform in order to achieve the goals that you want. For example, one of your goals is to save $2,000 in 6 months. Your discipline list will include things like; putting aside at least $350 every month and avoid spending money on unnecessary things like fancy restaurants or video games. High self-discipline in this example would be doing everything on that list without any exception. This does not mean that you cannot reward yourself or take a break from working towards your goals, it simply means that you should get the things done on your list before you indulge in any rewards.

2. Use a daily list to track your finances and to monitor unnecessary spending.

Make sure you are using a daily list to keep track of all the things that you need to get done in order to achieve your goals. Try to use online tools or just a simple notebook that can help you prioritize and organize. It feels very satisfying to be able to check off items that you've completed, and it will even motivate you to finish other tasks that are on your list just to feel the satisfaction of being able to check off another box. Make sure your to-do list works hand-in-hand with your discipline list to help yourself stay on track. A useful tip to keep in mind when you're feeling unmotivated is to start off with the easiest item on the list just to get the ball rolling. Once you complete one easy task, people normally feel more motivated than before; this will help you get started on the rest of your list. Starting with a harder task May create apprehension about doing it; therefore, start small and work your way up.

3. Figure out which obstacles are holding you back from success.

Different people have different things that distract them from being able to complete important tasks. For example, a person that is easily distracted by emails and people in their office might have to close their office door as soon as they get into work to get their own tasks done. They may delay any phone calls or meetings unless they're absolutely necessary in order to be able to complete their own set of responsibilities. This holds true for people that may be trying to lose weight. If they know that junk food is their weakness, instead of having to resist the temptation of eating junk food in their house, they can simply get rid of all the junk food in their house, so they don't have access to it. It is important that you minimize and remove all temptations of the distractions that affect you the most when it comes to reaching your most important goals.

4. Share your financial goals with other people.

For some people, it may be easier to stick with completing a goal when they have made a public commitment to it. The thought of failing to reach a goal in front of other people can be motivation for the person to stick with it. You can also take this one step further and ask those people to hold you accountable as well. If you aren't sharing your goals with anyone, nobody will know if you have been slacking off from it. When nobody is there to hold you accountable, you will likely be less motivated to keep doing it since nobody will know if you did fail at it.

5. Use external sources or motivation as well as internal.

There is a saying that goes, "don't do it for others; do it for yourself." However, some people find that they are much more disciplined when they know that their impulses, emotions, behaviors, and actions affect other people. Contrary to popular belief, it's alright to use external sources to help your motivation. In fact, sometimes, motivation coming from external sources is more powerful than internal motivation. Find the purpose that's beyond yourself that is important to you in order to help give you a higher chance of success.

6. Discipline is created by creating habits.

When something becomes a habit, you no longer need to draw from your will power bank to get yourself to do it. For example, if your goal was to stop spending money at restaurants for lunch during the workday, get into the habit of making yourself fulfilling meals to prevent yourself from buying food when you're at the office. You will be able to see the benefits of saving money if you are able to stick with it. Once you see the benefit, you will have more motivation to keep doing it, and soon it becomes a habit where it will feel strange to not be making your own meals. This way, you will no longer need to draw from your bank of self-control, but instead, meal-prepping will come naturally since it has become a habit of yours.

7. Stop making excuses.

Don't procrastinate, or wait for tomorrow, do it now. If you fall off the wagon, that's okay. Start over immediately. Stop telling yourself that something is too hard, or there's something that you cannot change. Don't blame other people for the circumstances that you're in. Making excuses is the Kryptonite of self-discipline. Achieve a mindset that is more about "I can do this" rather than, "I'll do it tomorrow."

Chapter 2: How To Build A Financially Intelligent Mindset

The most important thing about becoming a successful entrepreneur is your mindset. Your hard skills and network connections will never matter as much as the way you think and how you view yourself and your capabilities. To employ a financially intelligent mindset, you must improve yourself in four areas. These areas are:

- Self-discipline
- Habits
- Skills
- Procrastination

These areas work hand in hand to ensure that you are as productive as you can in the areas that matter the most. If you are lacking either one of these fundamentals, you can wave your ambitious dreams goodbye. This is the reason why not everybody can become a successful entrepreneur. Attaining these fundamentals takes a lot of work, time, and commitment. However, if you are able to dedicate yourself to building up these four fundamentals, you will begin to see changes in your life very quickly.

Let's talk a little about how self-discipline plays a role in helping you become a successful entrepreneur. A huge part of becoming successful, whether if it's in your career or personal life, is being able to be productive. In a world like ours today, where every day is filled to the brim with distractions, it is not easy to stay productive and not be distracted. Staying focused requires a lot of self-discipline, self-control, and willpower.

For instance, if your goal was to save $50,000 by the end of the year so you can invest it into your business, you have to properly manage your time so that you have enough energy and resources to complete tasks that will take you closer to your $50,000 goal. If you lack self-discipline and self-control, it will be easy for you to spend your money on attractive things like going on a vacation or buying yourself a new car. The act of self-discipline and employing that in all areas of your life is absolutely required when you are trying to achieve goals this large. In the later chapters of this book, you will be given the opportunity to learn about what self-discipline is and how you can learn and apply it to your life. Only with this, are you able to continue to develop yourself into being able to build the habits and routines that successful entrepreneurs have.

Using self-discipline, you are then developing the ability to foster other important aspects of becoming a successful entrepreneur. Mastering your self-discipline will allow you to build better habits that will ease your journey. Better habits such as improving time management, increasing persistence, and increasing organization will help you reach your goals quicker. Utilizing your newly developed self-discipline and habits, you will be able to translate that into the honing and development of new skills. People that have achieved significant success in their life have a set of skills that they are growing every single day. This will be no different for you.

Skills that entrepreneurs typically have include learning strong business acumen, money management, and a specialization in the industry they are in. By mastering skills in the area that you are planning to capitalize on will put you forward ahead of your competition. Later on in this book, I will teach you numerous ways to help you improve your existing skills and to master new ones quickly. One of the crucial things you have to understand before learning about developing and mastering new skills it that you must employ a growth mindset. If you are someone who has a fixed mindset – you will be faced with a tough time in terms of developing your skills. Changing your mindset from fixed to growth is a crucial step when it comes to learning and mastering new skills.

Your journey of becoming an entrepreneur and starting your own business begins with learning self-discipline. Once you begin applying the skills of self-discipline, you are able to build up other fundamentals like habits, skills, and mindset. We also have to keep in mind that a journey like this isn't one without hardship. The reason why not everybody has their own successful business is due to the fact that some people aren't able to move past their failures or overcome obstacles. That will be addressed in this book as well. One of the major obstacles that come between a person and their success is procrastination. Procrastination can be easily overcome with self-discipline; however, resisting temptations every single day makes it harder and harder for a person to overcome them due to the amount of energy and willpower it requires. Instead, I will be teaching you ways of avoiding procrastination and overcoming them. This will help you avoid procrastination, which requires less energy rather than having to overcome them every single time.

Overall, the concept and theory behind developing yourself into a person of success are fairly simple. Self-discipline, combined with better habits, skills, and mindset with the ability to overcome failures and obstacles, is the true recipe for success. I will teach you about all of these topics, theory and actual practice included, to lead you in the right direction.

Employing A Growth Mindset And Removing Your Fixed/Failure Mindset

Having a growth mindset is crucial in your journey of finding success. This is especially true if you want to become a successful entrepreneur as there will be many new skills and areas you will need to learn and improve on as you grow your business. The one thing that sets most people back from reaching their goals is not knowing how to deal with failures and adversity. When it comes to achieving your goals, you have to accept that failure is a part of the process. Don't fool yourself by believing that you won't face failure along the way. Everybody does, it's a part of the process. The difference between people who find success and those who don't is simple. Because those who did were able to learn from their failures, grow, and overcome it.

When you are faced with adversity, you must forgive yourself for any mistakes you have made and move forward. Famous snowboarder Mark McMorris, a multi-gold medal Olympian made a huge mistake that nearly cost him his life while snowboarding. Most people may have ended their athletic career right then and there in fear for their life. However, he persevered, healed, went through physiotherapy until he was well again.

This resulted in him winning more gold medals than ever before and is one of the most renowned athletes in the world. I hope that you never have to go through a life-threatening experience, but the point I'm trying to get across is that failures and mistakes are a part of the journey. Separate yourself from it and keep moving forward. Do what you can to grow and heal so you can come back stronger than before.

The 'growth mindset' is a term that was coined by Carol Dweck, who is a renowned professor at multiple universities, including Columbia University, Harvard University, and the University of Illinois. Her research with Angela Lee Duckworth stated that intelligence is not a key indicator of success. In fact, they believed that success depends on whether or not the person has a growth mindset. A fixed mindset is when a person believes that their intelligence and skills are a fixed trait. They have what they have, and that's it.

This makes the person highly concerned with what skills and intelligence they currently have, and they do not focus on what they can gain. Therefore, their activities are limited to the capacity that they think they have. However, those with growth mindsets understand that skills and intelligence is something that can be developed and learned throughout the course of their life. This can be done through education, training, or simply just even passion. They understand that their brain is a muscle that can be 'worked out' to grow stronger.

A very famous psychologist wrote a book regarding procrastination and determined that people can have one of two mindsets; either it is fixed, or they have a growth mindset. People that use a fixed mindset think that their abilities and skills cannot be changed and that they are permanent. They can only utilize their existing skills, talents, and intelligence and believe that those things cannot be further developed. Those that have a fixed mindset are under the belief that they are born with a certain set of skills without a way to improve their abilities. They believe that if a person has talent, that they do not require effort to gain success. They believe that talent is something that comes naturally. A fixed mindset is a dangerous thing because it hinders a person's ability to change, learn, grow, and to make positive changes.

Consequently, the growth mindset is one that allows a person to believe that skills, abilities, and intelligence are things that can be developed if you put in the hard work. They have the belief that a person's skills and talents are just their starting point. They believe that they are born with certain strengths, but there is no limit to what other strengths or goals they can accomplish if they put in the effort. The psychologist who studied this theory believes that people who procrastinate suffer from perfectionism and often have a fixed mindset. What this means is that these people avoid doing the tasks that they need to do because they are afraid of the potential chance of mistakes and that completing anything that's not 100% perfect. They idealize all their work to be absolutely perfect due to the belief that if a task is not 100% matched with their current skills/talents, then they will inevitably fail; therefore, they put this task aside for another time where they feel more ready or capable.

Knowing this, it is important that you employ a growth mindset. Every single skill you have and your intelligence can be improved by putting in the effort to do so. Famous public figures of success like Oprah Winfrey, Steve Jobs, and Bill Gates all employed a growth mindset by overcoming every obstacle that got in the way. Rather than succumbing to defeat, they worked and discovered innovative ways to overcome previous failures and found success at the end.

Think about what mindset you have right now. If you already have a growth mindset, you simply need to continue practicing it while being proactive about avoiding obstacles and overcoming failures. If you think you are someone with a fixed mindset, change it right now. Believe me when I tell you that intelligence and skills can be improved upon with time and hard work.

If you don't believe me, just try it. Pick a random skill. This could be knitting, programming, jogging, or anything that can be learned. Set goals for yourself and begin learning something new. If you are able to take something that you have zero skill in and become proficient in it, you have just proved to yourself that growth mindsets are real and fixed mindsets only hold you back from success.

Successful Entrepreneurs Are Disciplined And Do Not Rely On Motivation

When people think of successful entrepreneurs, they often think that they are constantly motivated to build their business. This is not true. Motivation doesn't just appear when you ask for it; in fact, it often lacks in many people.

People that have set large goals for themselves often have the wrong mindset where they think that they need to feel fully motivated before they start working on a task/job. This mindset is unrealistic. People's motivation often does not arrive until they have started that task and are beginning to see progress. When people see progress, they start to see the fruits to their labor, and they become even more motivated to keep working until they have completed their task. You might be wondering what about the motivation that is needed in order to start working altogether? The answer to this is that a person needs to have a good understanding of the 'why' and the vision of that particular job. Before you even begin working on it, you should know what the benefits are going to be. You would be surprised at how many people waste a lot of time doing work that actually does not need to be completed. Moreover, people should be using prioritization in order to get the most urgent and important work out of the way first. By understanding the benefits of completing a task or job, you will fully be able to estimate its importance. In terms of smaller tasks/jobs, simply understanding what the benefits are of completing that task should be enough for motivation. For larger tasks and jobs, it is important that you have a way to measure your progress so you can further gain motivation and confidence from your work.

Here is something I want you to try in terms of utilizing self-discipline and creating your own motivation. I want you to try to break down your goal of building a successful business into the smallest steps possible. This will help you generate willpower easier as your tasks are less daunting, and it will also help you create more motivation as you begin to complete them.

Here's an example: imagine that your goal is to make an additional $50,000 of revenue in your business. It is January and of a new year, and you have no idea where to begin. Your side business is an online store that sells artisan coffee beans. Here is how I would break down this seemingly 'large' task into one that is more manageable and easier to accomplish:

1. Start with drafting a business plan for the year. If your goal is to generate $50,000 of revenue from your business, break it down into monthly and weekly revenues. $50,000 distributed over 12 months is approximately

$4,200 per month. If your coffee beans sell for $40 per bag, this means you will have to approximately 104 bags of coffee per month or 26 bags of coffee per week.

2. Now that you have a monthly and weekly goal in mind, doesn't it sound less daunting? Now, take a look at your current business. How many bags of coffee are you selling per week? If you are averaging around 20 bags per week, you now know that you need to start selling at least 26 per week to reach your $50K goal. Your next step is to start coming up with strategies to upsell your existing clients or to market to new ones.

3. At this point in your business, it would be wise to expand and try to reach out to new customers. Research the best marketing strategy for coffee bean businesses and reach out to marketing agencies to get advice on this. If you feel like they are offering you a strong marketing plan, use it, and see how your results differ.

4. Analyze your results, are your sales increasing? If yes, then your marketing strategy is working. If your sales are staying the same or decreasing, then you know it is time to reevaluate your marketing strategy. Stay flexible, and don't just commit yourself to one plan. Be flexible and change your plans according to your circumstances.

5. Assess your business every single week. Are you meeting your sales by selling 26 bags per week? Are you exceeding it? By keeping track of how you're doing, you can adjust your business plan to meet your goals.

By following these steps, suddenly that one large task earning an additional $50,000 of revenue became much more manageable. Instead of thinking about that one large sum of money, you are starting with simply breaking it down to a weekly/monthly goal. From there, you can now work on your goal week by week and adjust your plan based on your experience. By taking things one step at a time, your mind becomes less overwhelmed.

Chapter 3: Successful Entrepreneurs Are Disciplined And Productive

Understanding what the psychology behind self-discipline is is extremely crucial as it will help you learn what the driving factors are behind it. Successful entrepreneurs are always people that are both disciplined and productive. Learning to improve your self-discipline by understanding its nature and driving force will help you become a more successful entrepreneur. One of the main factors that drive self-discipline is willpower. A common belief in people is that they think they can change their lives for the better if they simply could just have more willpower. If people had more willpower, everyone would be able to save responsibly for retirement, exercise regularly, stop procrastinating, avoid alcohol and drugs, and achieve all kinds of their noble goals. One survey that studied all Americans and their annual stress found that the majority of the participants reported that lacking willpower is the number one reason for not following the changes that they want for themselves.

Entrepreneurs that learn to improve self-discipline will find that their productivity has increased. With increased productivity, you are able to complete all your business-related tasks with extra time to take care of yourself. In this chapter, I will be teaching you more about self-discipline, willpower, delaying instant gratification, and self-control. I will also end this chapter with a case study about how self-discipline and willpower affect someone's financial decision making.

Using Your Willpower As A Resource

In the survey that we just mentioned, it was reported that the biggest obstacle when it comes to people achieving change was the lack of willpower. Even though many people often place blame upon the scarcity of their willpower for their unhealthy choices, they are still grasping on to the hope of being able to achieve it one day. Most people in this study also reported that they think willpower is something that can be taught and learned. They are absolutely correct. Some research has recently discovered many ways of how willpower can be strengthened with training and practice. On the contrary, some participants in the survey expressed that they think they would have more willpower if they had more free time to spare. However, the concept of willpower isn't something that increases automatically if a person has more time in their day. So that leads me to the next question, how can people resist when they are faced with temptation? Over the last several years, many discoveries were made about how willpower works by scientists all over the world. We will dive a little deeper into what our current understanding of willpower is.

Weak willpower isn't the only reason for a person to fail at achieving their entrepreneurial goals. Psychologists in the field of willpower have built three crucial components when it comes to achieving goals. They said that you first need to set a clear goal and then establish the motivation for change. They said the second component was to monitor your behavior in regards to that goal. Willpower itself is the third and final component. If your goal is similar to the following; stop smoking, get fit, study more, or stop wasting time on the internet, willpower is an important concept to understand if you are looking to achieve any of those goals.

The bottom line of willpower is the ability to achieve long term goals by resisting temporary temptations and urges. Here are several reasons why this is beneficial. Over the course of a regular school year, psychologists performed a study that examined the self-control in a class of eighth-grade students. The researchers in this study did an initial assessment of the self-discipline within the students by getting the students, their parents, and teachers to fill out a questionnaire. They took it one step further and gave these students the task of deciding whether they want to receive $1 right away or $2 if they waited a week. At the end of the study, the results pointed to the fact that the students that had better test scores, better school attendance, better grades, and had a higher chance of being admitted to competitive high school programs all ranked high on the self-discipline assessment. These researchers found that self-discipline played a bigger role than IQ when it came to predicting academic success. Other studies have found similar evidence. In a different study, researchers asked a group of undergraduate university students to fill out self-discipline questionnaires that will be used to assess their self-control. These researchers developed a scale that helped score the student's in relation to the strength of their willpower. They found that the students that had higher self-esteem, better relationship skills, higher GPA, and had less alcohol or drug abuse all had the highest self-control scores from the questionnaire.

Another study found that the benefits of willpower tend to be relevant well past university years. This self-control study was conducted in a group of 1000 people who had been tracked since birth to the age of 32. This is a long term study in New Zealand, where they wanted to learn more about the effects of self-control well into adulthood. They found that the people who had high self-control during their childhood grew up into adults that had better mental and physical health. They also had fewer substance abuse problems, criminal convictions, better financial security, and better money-saving habits. These patterns were proven even after the researchers had adjusted external influences such as socioeconomic factors, general intelligence, and these people's home lives. These findings prove why willpower is extremely important in almost all areas of a person's life.

Now that you have learned the importance of willpower and the role it plays in multiple stages of a person's life, let's define it a little further. There are many other names used for willpower that is used interchangeably; this includes; drive, determination, self-control, resolve, and self-discipline. Some psychologists will characterize willpower in even more specific ways. Some define willpower to be:

- The capacity to overcome unwanted impulses, feelings, or thoughts.
- The ability to resist temporary urges, temptation and delay instant gratification in order to achieve goals that are more long-term
- The effortful and conscious regulation of oneself.
- The ability to engage a "cool" cognitive system of behavior rather than a "hot" emotional system
- A limited resource that has the capability to be depleted

Delaying Instant Gratification

Delaying instant gratification is something that all entrepreneurs need to learn to do. Improving self-discipline will definitely help a lot with this. If entrepreneurs are unable to delay instant gratification, they may spend their money and time in all the wrong places causing the business to be unsuccessful. Let's learn a little more about this through a famous case study.

Over 40 years ago, a famous psychologist studied self-control within children using a simple and effective test. You may have seen this study used before in modern-day experiments. His experiment is called the "marshmallow test." This test has become extremely famous over the years as it laid the groundwork and then paved the way for modern studies of self-control.

This psychologist and his colleagues began the test by showing a plate of marshmallows to a child at the preschool age. Then, the psychologist let the child know that he had to go outside for a few moments and that he would let the child make a very simple decision. If the child could wait until the psychologist came back into the room, she could have two marshmallows. If the child could not or doesn't want to wait, then she can ring the bell, which then the psychologist would come back to the room right away, but then she would only get to have one marshmallow.

Willpower can be defined as simple as the ability for a person to delay instant gratification. Children who have high self-control are able to give up the immediate gratification of eating a marshmallow so that they can be able to eat two of them at a later time. People who have quit smoking sacrifice the satisfaction of one cigarette in hopes of having better health and lower the risk of cancer in the future. Shoppers fight the urge to spend money at a mall so they can save their money for their future retirement. You probably get the point here.

This marshmallow experiment actually helped the researchers develop a framework that explains people's ability to resist or delay instant gratification. He proposed a system that he calls "hot and cool" in order to explain whether willpower will succeed or fail. The 'cool' system is naturally a cognitive one. It means that it is a thinking system that uses knowledge about feelings, sensations, goals, and actions that remind oneself, for example, why the marshmallow shouldn't be eaten. The cool system is very reflective, while the hot system is more emotional and impulsive. The hot system is responsible for quick and reflex-based responses to specific triggers, for example, eating the single marshmallow without thinking about the long term ramifications. To put this in layman's terms, if this framework were a cartoon, the hot system would be the devil, and the cool system would be the angel on your shoulder.

When somebody's willpower fails, their hot system essentially overrides their cool system, which leads them to make impulsive actions. However, some people are more or less affected by the hot system triggers. That susceptibility to emotional responses plays a big role in influencing a person's behavior throughout life. The same researcher discovered that when he revisited his experiment with the children that had now grown up into adolescents, he found that the teenagers who were able to wait longer to have two marshmallows when they were children were more likely to have higher SAT grades and their parents were more likely to rate them of having better ability to handle stress, plan, respond to reason and exhibit self-control in frustrating situations and could concentrate better without being easily distracted.

Funnily enough, the marshmallow study didn't end there. A few other researchers tracked down almost 60 people who are now middle-aged, who had previously been a part of the marshmallow experiment as young children. These psychologists proceeded to test the participants' willpower strength using a task that's been proven to prove self-control within adults.

Surprisingly, the participants' various willpower strengths had been very consistent over the last 40 years. Overall, they found that the children who were not successful in resisting the first marshmallow did poorly on the self-control tasks as an adult and that their hot stimuli seem to be consistent throughout their lifetime. They also began to study brain activity in some of the participants by using magnetic resonance technology. When these participants were presented with tempting stimuli, those who had low willpower exhibited brain patterns that were very different from the brain patterns of those that had strong willpower. They discovered that the prefrontal cortex (this is the region of the brain that controls choice-making functions) was more active in the participants who had stronger willpower and the ventral striatum (an area of the brain that is focused on processing rewards and desires) showed increased activity in the participants who had weaker willpower.

Can You Run Out Of Willpower?

As an entrepreneur, you are likely exerting willpower and self-discipline all the time to ensure you are making the best decisions you can for your business. In this subchapter, you will be learning about the concept of willpower and whether or not it's possible to run out of it. The hot-cold framework does a great job of explaining people's ability to delay gratification, but there is another theory that is called 'willpower depletion' that has emerged in recent years to explain what happens to people after they have resisted multiple temptations. Everyone exerts willpower every day in one form or another. People resist to surf the web or go on social media instead of finishing their work report. They may choose a salad when they are craving a slice of pizza. They may hold their tongue rather than make a snide remark. Recent growing research indicates that resisting temptations takes a mental toll on a person. Some people describe willpower as a muscle that can get tired if overused.

The earliest discoveries of this concept came from a study that was conducted in Germany. The researcher brought participants into a room that smelled like fresh-baked cookies. The participants sat down at the table that held a bowl of radishes and a plate of those freshly baked cookies. The researchers asked some of the participants to taste those cookies while the others were asked to try the radishes. After this, the participants were assigned to complete a difficult geometric puzzle in 30 minutes. The researchers found that the participants who had to eat the radishes (therefore resisting the urge to eat the cookies) took 8 minutes to give up on the puzzle while the participants who got to eat the cookies tried to complete the puzzle for 19 minutes. The evidence here seems as if the people who used their willpower to resist eating the cookies drained their resources for future situations.

In the late 90s, this research was published, and since then, numerous other studies have begun looking into willpower depletion or otherwise known as ego depletion. One study, for example, the participants were asked to hold back and suppress any feelings they had while they watched an emotional film. These participants then participated in a physical stamina test but gave up sooner than the participants who watched the movie and reacted normally without any suppression.

Depleting willpower is very common in today's society. You have probably tried to make yourself be diplomatic when you are dealing with an aggravating customer or forced to fake happiness when your in-laws come to stay with you for an extended period of time. You must have realized that certain social interacts demand the use of willpower. There is also existing research that has proven that people interacting with others and maintaining relationships often is a high depleter of willpower.

Willpower depletion is not solely just a simple case of feeling tired. During another study by the same researcher, she had the participants in her study go through a whole day of sleep deprivation and then asked them to watch a movie but to suppress their emotions and reactions during it. She then proceeded to test the strength of the participant's self-control and found that those participants who didn't get sleep were not much more likely to be depleted of willpower compared to those who got a full night's sleep.

So if willpower isn't related to physical fatigue, then what exactly is it? Research studies have recently discovered a few different mechanisms that are possibly responsible for willpower depletion, some that were at the biological level. The researchers found that the people whose willpower became depleted after completing self-control tasks showed lowered activity in the region of their brain that controlled cognition. When willpower is being tested, a person's brain may begin to function differently.

Some other evidence indicates that people who have depleted willpower might be on low on fuel quite literally. Since the brain is an organ that requires high-energy that is powered by glucose, certain professionals suggested that the cells in the brain that are responsible for maintaining a person's self-control use up glucose quicker than it is being replenished. They performed a study with dogs where the dogs that were obedient and were asked to resist temptation showed lower blood glucose levels compared to the dogs that did not need to use self-control.

They found similar patterns in humans during scientific studies. The people who needed to use willpower in tasks were tested to have lower glucose levels compared to the participants that weren't asked to utilize their willpower. Moreover, replenishing glucose levels tend to help reboot a depleted willpower source in individuals that were depleted while drinking a sugar-free drink did not.

However, there is still evidence that suggests that the depletion of willpower can be maintained by a person's attitudes and beliefs. Different research and other colleagues found out that the people who felt the need to use their willpower (usually in order to please other people) were found to be more easily depleted compared to the people who are driven by their own desires and goals. These researchers, therefore, suggested that the people who are in better touch with themselves may be better off in life compared to the people who are often people-pleasing.

Some other researchers also studied how the effects of mood could affect a person's willpower. A study that took place in 2010 discovered that the group of people who believed that willpower is a resource that is limited were more likely to have willpower depletion. However, the group of people that did not believe that willpower can be depleted didn't show any symptoms or signs of willpower exhaustion after using their self-control. During the next stage of the same study, the psychologists manipulated the participants' subconscious beliefs by getting them to unknowingly fill out a biased questionnaire. The group that was manipulated to believe that willpower is for a fact a limited resource exhibited symptoms of willpower depletion/exhaustion while the group that believed that willpower was not depletable didn't show any signs of declining self-control.

Improving Self-Control

Entrepreneurs are people that require a whole lot of self-control. A ton of research has been developed recently in order to explain the numerous elements of willpower. Many professionals that study this area of self-control to this with one goal on their mind. They are about these types of questions: If willpower is a limited resource, what can we do to conserve it? How can we strengthen willpower?

One effective tactic for maintaining willpower is simply to avoid temptation. In the marshmallow study, children were given a choice of being allowed to eat one marshmallow right away or having to wait an undefined period of time to have the opportunity to eat two marshmallows. They found that the kids who started at the marshmallows during the whole time were found to be less likely to resist the treatment compared to the kids who shut their eyes and refused to look, looked away, or created a distraction for themselves. The technique of out of sight, out of mind, works with adults as well. In a recent study, researchers found that office workers who kept unhealthy snacks such as candy in their desk drawers consumed it less compared to when they would put the candy on top of their desks at eye level.

A technique called "implementation intention" is another helpful tactic that helps improve willpower. These intentions are usually in the form of "if-then" statements that aid people in planning for situations that are likely to disrupt their goals. For instance, a person that is monitoring their consumption of alcohol may tell themselves before entering a drinking part that is anybody offers them an alcoholic drink, then they will request a plain soda with lime. Research has found that amongst adults and adolescents, implementing solutions will increase self-control, even if people already had their willpower depleted by other tasks. People that have a plan ahead of time allows them to easily make decisions in the moment without needing to draw upon their bank of willpower resources.

This research suggests that people who have a bank of willpower that is limited raises a few troubling questions. Are people destined to fail if they are being faced with too many temptations? The answer is not necessarily. Many psychologists have the belief that a person's willpower cannot be ever used up completely. Instead, people often have stored some backup willpower that is being saved for future demands. Those reserves are only available for the right type of motivation, allowing them to accomplish things even when their willpower has seemingly run out.

In order to demonstrate this idea, a researcher further found out that individuals who had their willpower used up 'completely' continued to be able to accomplish self-control tasks when they were being told that they would be compensated well for their actions or if their actions would bring benefit to other people. He concluded that having high motivation can overcome weaken self-control.

Will power can also be controlled in the first place to be less vulnerable to being completely depleted. Psychologists often use an analogy to describe will power as being similar to a muscle that will tire out after a lot of exercise. However, there is another element to this analogy. Although muscles will tire due to exercise during the short-term, they become stronger when regularly exercised over the long term. Just like physical exercise, self-control can become stronger when a person exercises willpower.

According to one of the earlier experiments that supports the idea above, the researchers asked participants in the study to follow a two-week guide to improve their moods, track their food intake, or improve their physical posture. Compared to the group that didn't need to exercise self-control, the participants who had to use their willpower by performing heavy willpower exercises were not as vulnerable to the depletion of self-control in a follow-up study. In another set of research, this researcher found that smokers who exercised willpower for two weeks by avoiding sweet foods or regularly squeezing an exercise handgrip, found more success when it comes to not smoking than other participants who performed two weeks of tasks that didn't require any self-control.

Other researchers have also discovered that using your willpower muscles can help a person increase the strength of their self-control over a period of time. Some researchers in Australia did a study where they assigned participants to a physical exercise program that lasted two months; this is a willpower-required routine. In the conclusion of this program, the participants that finished it scored better when measuring self-control compared to the other participants who were not assigned the exercise program. The participants that did the program were also reported to have been smoking less, eating healthier food, drinking less alcohol, improving their study habits, and monitoring their spending habits more carefully. Regular exercise of a person's willpower using physical exercise seem to have led to an increase of will power in components of their daily lives.

The research findings regarding how glucose levels are tied to willpower depletion suggest a conceivable solution. A person that is maintains their blood sugar by eating regularly and often may help their brain replenish their storage of willpower—those who are dieting aim to preserve their willpower while calorie reduction may be more effective. You can do this by eating frequent and small meals compared to skipping out on entire meals like lunch or dinner.

All this evidence, founded from studies of the depletion of willpower, proposes that people making resolutions for the new year is the worst approach possible. If a person is running low on willpower in one specific area, it often reduces their willpower in all of the other areas. Focusing on one goal at a time makes more sense. In other words, don't try to get into a healthy diet right away, quit smoking, and start a new workout plan all at the same time. A much better technique is to complete goals one by one. Once you have one single good habit nailed, people no longer need to use their supply of willpower to maintain that behavior. Habits that are healthy will eventually become a part of a person's daily routine and would not need to use the energy of decision-making at all.

There are still many questions regarding the nature of willpower that needs to be answered by future research. However, it seems like if somebody has clear goals, good self-monitoring, and does a little bit of practice, they can train their self-control to be strong when faced with temptation.

Case Study On Willpower And Financial Decision Making

The temptation of consuming in materialistic things like new shoes or a new car is a test of willpower that we have all experienced. Just like how unhealthy food options have become plentiful, the opportunities for impulse spending has grown as well. ATMs are on every corner, and the rise of shopping online only allows a person to spend all their money without having to even leave the comfort of their couch. Willpower depletion affects people's ability to choose healthier lifestyle options and also affects their purchasing behavior.

Professors from the University of Minnesota did a study that focused on impulse buying and willpower depletion. They showed the participants a silent movie with a series of words that appeared on the bottom of the screen. A group of those participants was asked to not pay attention to those words, which were a task that required the use of self-control. After the movie, the participants were asked to look through a catalog with products like cars and watches, and they wrote down the money amount that they were willing to pay for every single item. The participants that used self-control during the movie were willing to spend more money, about $30,000, while the participants who didn't deplete their willpower were willing to spend approximately $23,000.

In the next experiment, the researchers tested the spending behavior of the participants by showing them the opportunity to buy lower-cost objects like cups and decorative stickers. The group that had done self-control in the previous experiment expressed that they felt a higher temptation to buy those items. In fact, They purchased more items and spent more money compared to the participants who hadn't done the self-control exercise.

The task of making decisions financially can be much harder for people that are impoverished. Researchers conducted various studies in India to explore the relationship between poverty and will power strength. In one study, this researcher visited two different Villages, one that was poor and one that was richer. The researcher offered people an opportunity to buy a luxury brand name soap at an extremely discounted price tag. This item was a great deal in terms of cost, but it still showed that people who live in poverty had difficulty making financial decisions as such.

The participants in the study were told to squeeze a handgrip made for exercise, which is a popular test of strength regarding self-control, before and after the soap was offered to be purchased. The researcher found that the participants who had more money exercised the handgrip for the same amount of time prior to and after the opportunity to buy that soap. However, they found that poor participants squeezed the handgrip for a smaller amount of time after making a purchasing decision. Their willpower was depleted, and the researcher had concluded that it was likely to run down by the difficulty of making that financial decision.

This research may sound depressing, but there is a silver lining. If impoverished people have a higher chance of using up their willpower, then it could possibly mean that lowering the number of hard decisions that they have to make every day to help prevent the depletion of willpower will give them the ability to make future decisions. A different researcher studied this effect amongst thanking customers in Southeast Asia. They offered customers the opportunity to open a savings account, but it comes with a catch. These customers would only be able to withdraw their funds after reaching a targeted saving goal or target date that they have decided for themselves. A year later, the participants that signed up for these accounts saved 82% more than the participants who had not opened the special savings account. When the decision to save money or spending money is taken away, it helps customers avoid failing at self-control.

All of this evidence collaborated to show that the people who are in the lower end of the socioeconomic spectrum are more likely to deplete their self-control resources. It's not that people who don't have money have less willpower than rich people; rather, the people that are living in poverty have to make more willpower draining decisions. This means that every decision they make, whether it is as simple as buying soap, will require self-control, which, therefore, dips into their limited resources of willpower.

Chapter 4: How To Achieve Self-Discipline For Entrepreneurs

With your new understanding of self-discipline and willpower, I will now be teaching you step by step on how you can achieve strong self-discipline to help you make better decisions and improve your productivity, related to your business. Regardless of whether it is your business you want to improve or just some areas of your personal life, self-discipline is the driving factor behind it all. Everyone faces difficult decisions when they are presented with temptations that are hard to resist. A person that is looking to eat healthier may struggle with their self-discipline when they are offered a hot fudge sundae. A person who is looking to gain some muscle mass may face a temptation of wanting to sleep in rather than going to the gym. People that have stronger self-control often spend less time thinking about whether or not to indulge in temptations that are bad for their health. Instead, they are able to make better decisions for themselves more easily. They don't let feelings or impulses affect their decision making. They are always able to make level-headed decisions.

Here are ten steps that you can follow to master your self-discipline as it related to entrepreneurship:

Step 1: Identify What Your Weaknesses Are

Everyone has their own set of weaknesses. As an entrepreneur, they could range from spending money on leisurely activities rather than investing in your business, or it could be as simple as choosing to play video games than to work in your business. Regardless of what it is, it has a similar effect on everyone.

The first step to mastering your self-discipline is to acknowledge your shortcomings, no matter what they might be. People often try to pretend that their weaknesses don't exist in order to portray themselves as a strong person. This is extremely ineffective when it comes to self-discipline. The purpose of acknowledging your weaknesses is not to make yourself feel bad; instead, it helps you recognize what they are and will help you plan in advance to overcome them. Acknowledge your flaws, and it is impossible to overcome them until you do this.

Step 2: Eliminate Your Temptations

Once you have acknowledged your weaknesses, you can now move on to step two, which is to remove your temptations. Just like we mentioned in step one, everyone has their own set of weaknesses, and it can range from small things like an unhealthy snack all the way to something that hinders your productivity like playing a video game for hours on end. By understanding what your weaknesses are, you can make accommodations for yourself that will help remove some of those temptations.

For example, if somebody is looking to lose weight and get fit at the gym, but they know that their weakness is that they always eat chocolate after dinner every night. Their temptation removal, in this case, would be to not buy any more chocolate that they keep around in their home. By not having chocolate in the home, they would be unable to fall into the temptation of eating it which will hinder their progress of getting fit. However, this does not mean that they will never be able to eat chocolate again. This only means that they can indulge in their favorite snacks when they have achieved a certain portion of their goal. Rewarding oneself is important to self-discipline, as well.

Step 3: Build A Business Plan With Clear Goals

In order to continue strengthening your self-discipline, a person must have a clear vision of what goals they are trying to accomplish. They must also have an understanding of what success means to them. If a person doesn't know where they're planning to go or what accomplishing their goals even and Tails, it is easy for them to lose their way or to get sidetracked.

Make sure the goals that you are setting have a clear and concise purpose. For example, don't use goals like "I want to be rich by the next five years." This goal is too broad for it to have a strong meaning. Instead, you should make a goal that is quantifiable like "I am planning on saving $20,000 by the end of this year". Then, when you have a quantifiable goal, you are able to make a plan that makes sense for yourself. In this example, a person can plan to save $2,000 each month for the rest of this year in order to hit their goal of saving $20,000 by the end of it. They can break down these goals even further, and figure out where in their budget they can save money or how they can make more money to accomplish that goal.

Step 4: Train Your Self-Discipline Every Day

Self-discipline is not something that people are born with; it is mostly a learned behavior. Self-discipline is just like any other skill that people may be looking to grow; it requires repetition and lots of daily practice. Similar to going to the gym, the more you work out your muscles, the bigger and stronger they will become. Changes do not happen overnight, instead to strengthen your muscles and to grow them, it will take at least several weeks for a person to be able to see their progress. The effort and focus that training self-discipline requires can be extremely tiring.

The more time you practice self-discipline, it can become more and more difficult to keep utilizing your willpower. Sometimes when a person is faced with a big temptation or decision, they may feel that overcoming that large temptation makes it harder for them to overcome other tasks that also require self-discipline. The only way to move past this is to have a good mindset. By having a good mindset, it creates a buffer for how quickly your willpower becomes drained. In addition, like the muscle example we used, by exerting your willpower more often, you will have a higher tolerance and therefore be able to exert it more than if you were just starting out.

Step 5: Build Simple And Healthy Habits

To strengthen self-discipline, you need to work on instilling a new habit, which can feel very intimidating at first, especially if you are focusing on the entire goal all at once. To avoid this daunting feeling, keep it very simple. Break your bigger goal into smaller doable ones. Instead of trying to accomplish one huge goal all at once or to change all of your habits all at once, focus on doing just one thing consistently and exercise your self-discipline with that one small thing.

For example, if you are somebody that is looking to get into better shape, start by exercising for 10 to 15 minutes per day. Instead of trying to go to the gym for 2 hours every day, which can be very daunting, start with a smaller goal in mind first. By taking baby steps, you can get your mind used to that habit and slowly increase the amount of time that you spend at the gym. Eventually, once you feel like that goal has become a habit, you can then begin to focus on other small goals and keep building up words from there.

Step 6: Implement A Healthier Lifestyle

Eating well affects people more than they think. We learned in the earlier chapters that glucose levels play a big role in a person's brainpower, which controls a person's willpower. The sensation of being hungry can cause people to feel angry, annoyed, and irritated. This feeling is real and everyone has felt it before and often has a huge impact on a person's willpower. Research has found evidence that having low blood sugar weakens a person's ability to make good decisions.

When a person is hungry, their ability to concentrate suffers a lot, and their brain doesn't function as optimally. Therefore, a person's self-control is likely to be weakened when their body is in this state. To prevent this, make sure to be eating small meals constantly to prevent yourself from feeling that annoying hungry feeling that causes people to have a lapse in judgment. Since exercising willpower takes up a lot of energy from a person's brain, make sure to keep fuelling it with enough glucose so that the brain is able to keep functioning at an optimal level.

Step 7: Change Your Views On Willpower

We learned in the earlier chapters that a person's point of view or their beliefs can create a buffer of how long it takes to have their willpower drained completely. Although most researchers believe that there is a limit to how much we can tap into our willpower, they also found that the people who believe that there wasn't a limit had a bigger will power stockpile. If a person believes that they have a limited amount of willpower, they probably will not be able to surpass those limits. However, if a person does not place a strict limit on themselves, they are less likely to use up their willpower stockpile before meeting their goals.

A person's internal perception about their own willpower and self-control plays a huge role in determining how much willpower they have. If a person can remove these obstacles by believing that they have a large stockpile of willpower, and believing in themselves, then they are less likely to drain out there will power compared to someone who believes that they don't have much of it. So try changing your own perception of how you see your willpower. Try to think of it as a source that can run out, but because of your beliefs, you have a larger amount of it. This is a much better mindset to be in compared to thinking that willpower will run out, so therefore you should be stingy with it.

Step 8: Create A Backup Plan

Many psychologists use a famous technique that helps with boosting willpower called "implementation intention." This technique is where you give yourself a plan when you are faced with a potentially difficult situation. We used this example earlier; if a person is trying to reduce the amount of alcohol that they drink and they know that they are going to a party where they will be asked if they want to drink alcohol, instead of always asking for a beer like they normally do, they will instead ask for a plain soda with lime.

By making a plan before going to a situation that you know where you will be confronted with big temptations, you will have an action plan in place where you can automatically use rather than having to come up with an excuse on the spot and risking failure. When a person goes into those situations with a plan, it helps give them the mindset and the self-control that is necessary to overcome obstacles. They will be able to save energy by not having to make sudden decisions or make sudden plans based on their emotional state. This will make them less likely to cave into temptations and more likely to exercise their self-discipline.

Step 9: Reward Yourself When You've Achieved

Just like anything else in life, it is necessary to give yourself a break and to give yourself a reward. Give yourself something to look forward to by planning an appropriate reward when you accomplish your goals. This is not much different from when you were a little kid, and you got a treat from your parents for showing good behavior. When a person has something to look forward to, it gives them the extra motivation that they need to succeed.

Anticipation is a powerful thing. It gives people something to focus on so that they are not only thinking of all the things that they need to change. When you have achieved one of your goals, you can find yourself a new goal and a new reward in order to keep motivating yourself to move forward. However, the reward should not be something unhealthy. For example, in the previous example of the person that is trying to lower their alcohol intake, their reward for not drinking as often should not be that they will go binge drinking next Friday. Their award should be something healthy that won't make them lose progress on all the work that they've done. As an entrepreneur, if you are celebrating your first sale, don't spend hundreds of dollars on a party as that will take resources away from your business. Instead, go for a nice dinner or have a gathering at your home.

Step 10: Forgive Your Mistakes And Move On

Even if a person has all the best intentions and the most well-made plans, sometimes they will fall short when practicing self-discipline. Avoiding failure altogether is impossible, and we should not build a mindset around that. Everyone will have their ups and downs, their successes, and their failures. The key to overcoming the failures that you will face is simply to keep moving forward. If you stumble on your journey of self-discipline, instead of giving up altogether, acknowledge what caused it, learn from it, and then move on. Don't let yourself get caught up in frustration, anger, or guilt because these emotions are the ones that will de-motivate you and get in the way of your future progress. Learn from the mistakes you have made and be comfortable with forgiving yourself. Once you have done that you can get your head back in the game and start where you left off.

Chapter 5: How To Build Healthy Habits For Entrepreneurs

Entrepreneurs who have successful businesses all have ten habits in common. These habits help them live a more well-rounded life that improves their productivity, discipline, and overall drive. In this chapter, I will teach you the ten habits that successful entrepreneurs have so you can begin implementing them into your life. In addition, I will also teach you about how habits are formed. Understanding the science behind how habits are formed will help you better understand what you need to do to solidify these habits into your life. Let's first start with learning about how habits are formed.

How Are Habits Formed?

Why is it so hard for people to stick to their new good habits for a certain amount of time before they give up and go back to their old ways? The huge problem in this, especially with old habits that have been there for years, are the neural pathways that have been imprinted into people's brains. This happens on a biological level. These neural pathways are responsible for linking up the neural networks in a person's brain to perform a specific function like pouring a cup of tea in a certain way, walking up the stairs, or smoking a cigarette.

These neural pathways created by our habits help us reduce the energy needed for the conscious processing power in a person's brain by automating certain behavior. By doing this, it allows a person's mind to focus on other things rather than the habitual tasks that they have done a thousand times. This automation function came from the beginning days of human life as a part of our DNA. It allows us to have a mind that is efficient and can be used for more important tasks rather than mundane things in our lives. The main difference between successful people and those who aren't is that they haven't mastered the art of forming these neural pathways for tasks that are beneficial towards your professional development.

In most scenarios, the things that often hold people back from building good habits are the mundane things we are used to repeating. More often than not, people tend to have automated more bad habits than good habits, which adds negative value to their life that causes them to achieve their goals slower, if at all. Since the cause of this is the neural pathways that get ingrained deeper and deeper over time, it makes it harder for people to break their bad habits or even form good ones when all of the bad ones are constantly getting in the way. However, if you can try to ingrain the next following habits we will be discussing into your life, you will find that strengthening your self-discipline may become easier. Again, these things don't happen overnight. Keep in mind that habits take a long time to break and to form. It is important to start small and build new habits slowly as neural pathways do not get ingrained overnight. It will require repetition for many weeks to months before your brain automates these tasks. Discipline is very necessary for the initial stages of building a habit; however, if done correctly, it will be able to pay off for the rest of your life. Let's take a look at ten habits that all millionaire's likely to have, that you should start building to become more successful.

Habits That Financially Intelligent Entrepreneurs Have

The habits that I will be teaching you will range from incorporating exercise all the way to increasing your grit. Entrepreneurs face all types of adversity, so having higher energy levels and a stronger mindset will help you overcome the obstacles that will be thrown at you.

Habit #1: Time Management

If you are looking to become an entrepreneur to build wealth for yourself, you must maximize your use of time. Spending most of your time doing things that don't add to your future will only slow down or stop the process of you gaining the success that you want. In order to properly build wealth, whether that's by developing and honing a new skill or if it's managing your finances better, you must be able to manage your time properly so you are able to put the effort in the right places. An average person has to work at least 40 hours per week, all hours outside of that are limited, so time management is crucial.

When people are able to properly manage their time, they will begin to have room to do the things that actually matter. Mainly, they must make room to do the activities that they need in order to achieve the goals that they have set. In order for a person to achieve their long-term goals, they have to break it down into smaller daily goals that may not be the most urgent but are definitely still very important. If a person does not have good time management, they likely cannot even get the most urgent things that they need to get done in a day, let alone achieving goals that don't require immediate urgency.

To effectively measure if certain things are urgent, non-urgent, important, not important, you need to take a moment to think about whether or not the action that you are doing is not ·urgent but important· or ·not urgent and not important· or ·urgent and important.· The things that fall into the ·not urgent and not important· category are known as things that are time-wasters. This includes things like browsing social media on your phone or binge-watching your favorite Netflix series. Things that fall into the category of ·not urgent but important· are likely the short-term goals you have set for yourself. Although they don't need to be urgently completed, they are still important for your self-growth. Most of the tasks that you will be doing to move you closer to becoming a millionaire will fall under this category. Things that are urgent and important are likely deadlines or any responsibilities that you have to complete for your work.

A person's ability to strengthen self-discipline comes from their time management abilities. Some of the most successful people in the world are incredible time managers because, rather than using time as a detractor, they use time as a benefit. Everybody has the same amount of time in a day; we shouldn't waste it. Start managing your time by categorizing the things you need to do in a day with the categories I gave you above. Start by doing the things that are both urgent and important, then move on to the things that are not urgent but important. Leave the things that are both not urgent or important to the end of the day when you have completed all the other things. By doing this, you are maximizing your time for activities that are most beneficial to your growth.

Habit #2: Grittiness/Persistency

When it comes to building your own business and becoming successful, grit and persistence are crucial. No amount of self-discipline would ever be complete without the presence of persistence. Persistence is a type of habit that helps us to not give up even when we are faced with failure. Persistence is what helps us get back up on our feet to keep trying even when we do fail. Persistence plays such a huge role in self-discipline that without it, achieving self-discipline is probably impossible.

You might be wondering why that is. This is because achieving our goals is not an easy thing to do. It is really hard. Getting discouraged is easy and something that happens to everyone along their journey. In addition, the act of giving up requires less energy in comparison to being gritty and pushing through, even if it's a task that may cause pain in the process before any pleasure is returned. Successful entrepreneurs did not get to where they are by giving up when faced with hardships.

However, this hardship that is required to achieve any goals is simply something that you have to persevere through. We all have to understand that some of the most successful people in the world have experienced failure numerous times over and over again. Failure is simply a part of life, and rather than avoiding it and not pursuing your goals at all in fear of failure, we should learn to persevere and push through even during the hardest of times. Without failure, we wouldn't be able to reach our goals.

There are a variety of ways that a person can go about instilling perseverance as a habit, but the best and most effective weight is to come up with the reasons why you want to do the things in life that you aim for. If the reasons behind your goals are strong enough, they can motivate you so you can get through anything. The next time you are faced with an obstacle, rather than falling back onto your automatic bad habits of giving up, try something new and push through it. Get creative and problem solve; this will take you closer to achieving the goals you have never before.

Habit #3: Organization

Have you ever noticed that if your workspace is cluttered or messy, it makes it very hard to be concentrate, which leads you to be unfocused and distracted? Naturally, humans don't like living in a dirty and messy environment. In order for a person to achieve their goals and accomplish self-discipline, they need to be organized and feel organized. Organization also needs to become a habit that is fully incorporated in a person's personal life and professional life. This includes the physical act of organizing the things you have in your home and the mental act of organizing the things on your mind.

By living an organized life, you are fostering self-discipline. If you are someone who is constantly scattered and disorganized, start small with when building up your organization. Start with picking one small space each day for yourself to organize. This can be just one single drawer in your kitchen, the things lying around on your desk, or just straighten out the things on your coffee table. The next day, pick something else to organize like your bathroom drawers or the clothes in your closet. The more time you spend living in a clean and organized environment, the less you would want your home to become cluttered and messy again. You will start to begin to notice when clutter builds up, and by having a habit of organization, you will immediately organize things as you use them, so you don't have to spend time organizing it later on.

By de-cluttering your home or your working environment, you will have plenty of different areas where you can sit down and work on your own goals. Has your home ever been so cluttered that when you do have the motivation to start working on something, you simply just don't have the space to do it? In order to avoid this, keep your home clean and organized at all times so that when you have a rush of motivation, you can find a workspace that is clean and ready for you to work.

Similar to many other habits, organizational habits can be easily learned and reinforced over time. It does require your attention and effort, but it is something that will pay off tremendously in the future. When you are living in a physical space that is organized and clean, your mind will automatically become more stress-free, relaxed, and give you the ability to focus. In turn, by becoming more organized, you are increasing your ability to be more self-disciplined. Begin to incorporate this good habit of putting things back where it belongs when you're finished using it instead of leaving things where you last used it. Small things like this that we habitually do on a day to day basis impacts our quality of life heavily.

Habit #4: Frequent Exercise

Not only is exercise one of the cornerstones of living a healthy life in general, but it is also one of the most important habits to build within all people. It is a fundamental habit to help a person's life be filled with positive habits and be rid of the bad ones. A person that is truly able to discipline themselves has to instill the habit of exercise into their everyday routine. As you may already know, there are endless benefits when it comes to exercise. This is something that is talked about not only by psychologists but medical experts as well. Even though exercise is such an important component of a person's life, not everyone actually makes it a priority. Why is this?

As our lives get increasingly busy in the modern-day, everyone is caught up with trying to get all the things that they need to get done and are often busy running around completing errands and fail to incorporate exercise into their routines. Often, people have a bad mindset when it comes to exercise and think that they won't be able to build it as a habit because they simply have "too many other things to do." Especially if one of your goals is to become successful, many people think that exercise will take time away from completing other ·more urgent· tasks. This is where most people are wrong. There are ways to incorporate exercise even if their day is jam-packed from beginning to end. In fact, it will help you become more productive and efficient when achieving goals.

When people think of exercise, they may automatically think of a minimum one-hour intense weight-lifting session at the gym, a one-hour long, expensive spin class, or a one-hour yoga class. If that's what they are thinking about then yes, it is true that the people that have busy lives may not be able to incorporate the time to get to their exercise class, the time it takes to complete the exercise class, and then get to wherever they need to go after that. However, exercise doesn't necessarily have to be a formalized session that takes a long time. It can simply be getting some sit-ups, push-ups, or some jumping jacks in the morning before you head to work. It can also be you choosing to walk to work instead of taking the bus, or it could be a brief walk around your neighborhood park after dinner.

Begin by starting to build exercise habits in your daily routine by starting with an easy 10-minute walk or just doing some sit-ups and push-ups right after you wake up. Attempt to do this for one week and then increase the amount of time you spend on that session for the next week. Keep up with this pattern, and soon enough, you will have a healthy amount of time every day that you set aside to get your exercise in, and this is when it will become a full-blown habit.

When you are able to implement exercise as a keystone habit of your life, it can help you increase self-discipline and can also improve other areas of your life. First of all, exercise is extremely effective in reducing stress levels and pain because it causes the brain to release feel-good endorphins and neurotransmitters like serotonin and dopamine. Secondly, exercise helps increase the oxygenation and blood flow of body cells, which is responsible for helping boost the immune system and fighting off diseases. Lastly, exercise increases a person's ability to focus on a present task due to the increased activity in the brain, which allows us to live a life with more discipline.

Habit #5: Proper Sleep

According to the theory we learned earlier in this book about willpower, we learned that willpower requires energy from the brain, which gets its energy from glucose levels and rest. Based on this theory, it is safe to assume that sleep is directly connected to how the brain is able to acquire energy. When a person doesn't get enough sleep, their brain spends most of its energy focused on just keeping your basic body functions up and going. This does not leave much energy for a person to spend on exerting their willpower, practicing self-discipline, or even simply just remembering their self-discipline, ensuring that you get the right and a healthy amount of sleep is a crucial requirement for accomplishing anything. When a person doesn't get the right amount of sleep, it affects one's ability to focus, their judgment, their mood, their overall health, and their diet.

When people suffer chronic sleep deprivation such as insomnia, things go from bad to worse. Many research studies have found evidence that people who don't get enough sleep on a day to day basis are put at a higher risk of catching specific diseases. Not sleeping enough also has a significant and negative effect on a person's immune system. This can cause a person to frequently catch colds or flu that cause them to not have the ability to go to school, work, or get anything effective done. It is necessary to keep your body in good health in order to be productive. Constantly being sick or feeling unhealthy will simply make it harder for you to complete tasks that help you achieve your goals and may cause you to give in to temptation easier than if you had a healthy body and mind.

For most adults, get at least six hours of sleep every night. Ideally, you should be sleeping 8 – 10 hours per day. Avoid eating or drinking anything with caffeine in it before you go to bed to avoid it, affecting your sleep cycle. Make a note to also avoid ingesting a large number of toxins during your day like; cigarettes, alcohol, drugs, or prescription medicine if avoidable.

If you are able to improve sleep, you will gain extraordinary benefits. Benefits include; longer periods of time of staying focused and being more disciplined, minimizing pain and inflammation, reducing stress, improving memory, sharpening attention, improving your work quality, limits your chances for accidents, and helps you avoid depression.

Habit #6: Healthy Diet

Eating healthy is as important as exerting perseverance. If you are not eating a healthy diet, you are actually preventing yourself from reaching your full potential. What a lot of people don't realize is that our human body spends a huge portion of its energy digesting and processing food.

Healthy foods that you should be eating more of are raw fruits and vegetables. Raw fruits and foods give us the biggest boost of energy for humans because they use less energy for the body to process and provides higher energy levels for us to use after that. This process is called an enhanced Thermic Effect of Food (TEF) or otherwise known as Dietary Induced Thermogenesis (DIT).

According to what we learned earlier in this book, the human brain uses up a large amount of glucose in order to keep it functioning. Therefore, the amount of energy that a person has is responsible for how focused they feel when doing work. When a person is focused, they can achieve their goals using less willpower and time than if they weren't focused. When a person is running on low energy due to consuming foods with empty calories, staying focused will be very hard to achieve. People will often waste a lot of time sitting around or 'resting' as they feel too sluggish and tired to work on achieving their goals.

One of the most commonly heard things is that breakfast is the most important meal of the day. Although breakfast is important, it is just as important to eat multiple times per day and not just only eating breakfast. By ensuring healthy meals every part if the day, start by actively planning your meals to avoid falling into bad habits. For example, if you are planning to eat five healthy smaller-sized meals per day, but you haven't prepared any of those meals, you are more likely to feel hungry and indulge in unhealthy conveniences like fast food. Prepare your five healthy meals beforehand by meal prepping to ensure that you don't fall into eating unhealthy conveniences.

The food that we put into our body can change the neural chemical makeup of the human brain. It also plays a huge role in a person's mind and body connection. Take some time to assess the foods that you eat throughout your day. Identify the meals where you often consume the unhealthiest foods. Make an effort to plan in advance so you can substitute those meals with raw, organic, and healthy foods.

Habit #7: Frequent And Active Goal Setting

If your main goal is to build your own successful business, then you must actively set and adjust all smaller goals along the way that will help you achieve your main goal. Keeping your goals stagnant or refusing to break them down into smaller milestones will not only overwhelm you but can easily demotivate you.

Let's learn the difference between active goal setting and a passive goal setting. Passive goal setting means you are setting goals mentally, which makes them passive because of the lack of details involved. It also means that a person hasn't properly defined their actual goal, which makes causes difficulty when it comes to tracking progress and identifying the tasks that need to be done in order to achieve that goal. On the other hand, active goal setting is the complete opposite of passive goal-setting. Active goal setting means writing out your goals and ensuring an important meaning behind it. Active goals are measurable and specific. To successfully create and make an active goal, you must build a plan towards achieving it. This includes breaking down your goals into smaller tasks and steps that are clear and achievable.

By implementing active goal-setting into your daily life, it ingrains the discipline in us because you are forced to give it direction. By breaking down your big goals into smaller daily goals, it helps people avoid distractions by only looking at the things that they need to get done in the present day. This way, a person isn't left constantly thinking about one large intimidating goal but not knowing how to approach it.

Active goal setting works by taking the first step in setting your long-term goals. If you currently have long-term goals, then you need to actively participate in daily, weekly, and monthly goal setting and planning. You have to play an active role in tracking your progress towards your goals and making changes in places where you feel like you aren't working for you. Rather than just saying that your goal is to become a successful entrepreneur, you need to start planning exactly what steps you believe will take you there.

My advice for you will be to take out a pen and a piece of paper and start writing down what long-term goals you have. Once you have some long-term goals written down, break it down into monthly, weekly, and daily goals. Simply start off by accomplishing your daily goals, and when you reach the end of the month, assess to see if you have achieved your monthly goal through accomplishing your daily goals. If you haven't, look back on your daily goals and see if there's anything you can change so that you could achieve next month's goal.

Habit #8: Gratitude

Building a habit of gratitude may not be a habit that you would think contributes to one success. However, gratitude is an important feeling and practice in human life that helps not only people with self-discipline but is often used to help people that are facing self-esteem and self-confidence issues. A huge problem in our modern world today is that we are constantly presented with millions of materialistic things that cause us to always be wanting something more or something else. This causes people to spend too much time thinking about all the things that they want, and not enough time thinking about the things that they already have. Building a habit of practicing gratitude helps people stop thinking about wanting the things that they don't have and move forward towards appreciating the things that they do have. When people do this, they can begin to make changes in their life that truly matters.

The effects of practicing and showcasing gratitude are extremely crucial to fostering success. It does everything from improving mental health, emotional well-being, a person's spirituality, gratitude is capable of so many things. Practicing gratitude is an exercise that is constantly used in therapy to help the client move away from thinking about things that aren't in the present and focus on being mindful. Ultimately, gratitude helps people move away towards a state of abundance and away from a state of lack. When people live in a state of lack, it makes it impossible for them to focus on achieving their goals and being self-disciplined. They spend too much of their mental energy and capacity worrying about the things that they don't have or living in a fearful way, to the point that they forget about the things that they do have.

The state of lack can also show up in someone as physical symptoms. This state produces a lot of stress because the brain automatically releases cortisol and epinephrine, which are the stress hormones from our brains. These hormones impact numerous systems within the human body. When someone is stressed, their immune systems, digestive systems, and reproductive systems are all affected. When this happens, you have to spend more time and energy recovering your body rather than using your resources to achieve your goals. Start by practicing gratitude by writing down ONE thing that you are grateful for in your day. This will help you put your mind at ease and to give you some more perspective about the world.

Habit #9: Forgiveness

Have you ever caught yourself feeling angry or impatient over the smallest matter? This is because of the large amount of convenience we are offered in our daily lives. A simple annoyance that occurs in your day can cause a spiral of negative emotions. For example, if you are in a hurry to get to work and you happen to be running late that day, the coffee shop that you normally stop at to get your morning coffee is taking forever to make your order. When you finally get your coffee, you realize that they had made your order wrong, but now you have no time to get it fixed. That one simple human error has sent you into a spiral of anger and annoyance, and you struggle to let go of it, and you find that it is still negatively impacting your whole day. This causes you to have spent most of your energy upset about the coffee shop that wronged you, and you don't have enough mental capacity to focus on other things like practicing your self-discipline. When people spend most of their days feeling the emotions of anger, regret, or guilt, they actually are creating more problems than they are with solutions. The emotions of anger and hate consume much more energy in a person's body compared to positive emotions like forgiveness and love. Forgiveness is something that can be learned. When people learn to forgive, only then will they be able to let go of negative things they have been holding on to.

If you are aren't able to practice forgiveness in all areas of your life, to yourself and to others, you will have a hard time achieving true self-discipline. When an individual is constantly worried about how someone or something has wronged them, it makes it impossible for them to focus their energy on tasks and things that truly matter. If someone has hurt you in the past, start to try and learn how to forgive them. This does not mean at all that you have to forget about what they did to you altogether. Simply just forgive and let go of that negative energy and give it back to the universe rather than keeping it within your body. When we perform the act of forgiveness, we are actually letting go of the negative energy that inhibits our ability to practice self-discipline. If you want to master self-discipline, you have to get rid of sources that are sucking away at your mental energy. Holding on to negative emotions like anger is a sure way for your energy to be drained. While forgiveness might not seem like a discipline habit when you first look at it, it is an extremely crucial one to build in the process.

To start practicing your forgiveness habit, try to think of any people or situations that you are currently angry with. This can be someone that has wronged you in the past or a situation that affected you. Instead of just thinking about how it made you feel, try to put yourself in their shoes. What would be the things that you would do if you were in their situation? Make it light-hearted and try to find some humor in it. Rather than thinking about it as a situation that shouldn't have happened, try to think of a lesson that you have learned from those situations. I know that it is very hard to forgive certain people, especially if they have really hurt you or wronged you in life. However, it isn't until people are able to move on from feelings of animosity and hurt where their life actually begins to see some improvement.

Habit #10: Meditation

Similar to the effects of practicing gratitude, meditation is a commonly used technique to help people practice mindfulness in cases where they are suffering from feelings of anxiety and/or depression. Meditation is something that can be used to help put people's minds at ease. When people practice meditation, they take their awareness away from things of the past and the future and focus it on the things of the present. When this happens, they are able to connect themselves to the universe, which also helps them with increasing gratitude.

When you are able to maneuver your mind to stay in the present moment, you will give yourself room to think about the tasks at hand and not predict problems of the future. By doing this, it plays into improving your time management and overall productivity.

There are many types of meditation, some of which focuses on mindfulness and some of which focus on love and gratitude. There truly are too many different types of meditation for humankind to keep track of, but the most popular and beneficial type that is used amongst many therapies and within self-discipline is mindfulness meditation. Contrary to common belief, meditation only requires ten to fifteen minutes of time and doesn't need to be for hours on end. However, the hardest part of meditation is actually bringing yourself to do it. A person has to be able to keep their mind still and train it to stop wandering all the time. The trick behind mindfulness meditation is not to stop wandering thoughts altogether, but simply to acknowledge these thoughts and reroute yourself back to the present. There are many types of breathing techniques that can be accompanied with meditation to help with achieving mindfulness. You will have the chance to learn about using meditation in the next chapter.

Chapter 6: How To Improve Your Financial And Business Skills

The ability to quickly learn new skills and improving existing ones is crucial to entrepreneurs. With hundreds of thousands of new businesses being built every year, your ability to adapt and to learn new things will make or break your personal business. According to the growth mindset, anyone is capable of learning and mastering any skills they like as long as they truly believe they can do it. By putting in hard work and time, anyone can pick up a new set of skills. In this chapter, I will be teaching you about two strategies; the visualization strategy and meditation strategy. The visualization strategy is mainly used to practice certain skills to help you quickly master them. For instance, if you own a furniture-making company, you can practice your craftsmanship using visualization without actually needing to spend a ton of money on materials and equipment to practice. The meditation strategy will also help you as it will encourage you to plan out your business and all your goals into small tasks for you to achieve. This will make your goal and business feel less overwhelming and thus, lowering the risk of fear and procrastination. It will also help you achieve goals and milestones faster. Let's learn about visualization first.

Strategy #1: Visualization

Visualizing an action or a skill before actually performing it is nearly as powerful as physically performing that action in reality. Scientific studies have found evidence that people's thoughts actually produce the same instructions in their mind as it does with actions. This means that when somebody is mentally rehearsing or practicing something in their mind using the visualization process, it actually impacts the many cognitive processes within a person's brain that includes planning, motor control, memory, and attention perception.

In layman's terms, the way a person's brain is stimulated when they are visualizing an action is exactly the same as when they are actually performing it physically. Therefore, scientists can safely assume that the act of visualization provides just as much value as physically performing a task.

Many athletes in certain sports use the act of visualization to help themselves train before a competition. For example, in Olympic cycling, the cyclist will prepare for a competition by closing their eyes and visualizing the racetrack in their mind. They move their bodies while visualizing the way that they will travel through the racetrack in order to train their muscle memory and reflexes even further. This way, when they do begin to compete on the racetrack, they have already visualized themselves cycling through it using the strategies that they have been taught and visualized in their minds. This is a technique and training skill that many professional coaches teach their athletes to do.

When a person is visualizing, their conscious mind is aware that what they're visualizing is not real but is just a result of imagination. Consequently, a person's subconscious isn't able to differentiate the difference between what a person is thinking and what they are actually doing. In other words, a person's inner-mind isn't able to distinguish the difference between real life, a photo, past memories, or an imagined future. Rather, the mind is under the impression that everything a person sees is real. This is proven by numerous brain scans that scientists have conducted over the years, where they discovered that there are no brain activity differences when someone is observing something in the real world compared to when a person is visualizing.

All of this evidence is extremely important because it points the theory that visualization can help people learn new skills and be able to reprogram and rewire their brains without having to perform physical actions. For example, if somebody is looking to increase their self-esteem, they can use the process of visualization by imagining themselves doing those actions before actually doing it in the real world.

Visualization is often used by athletes to improve their technique in their sport. However, visualization can also be used to improve mental and emotional skills to reduce negative thinking and anxiety. It also helps a person improve their overall self-discipline, which we know is extremely important to entrepreneurs. By using the technique of working through scenarios in a person's mind can help them effectively require their brain in order to build new patterns, habits, and behaviors, which makes completing tasks in the real world far less anxiety-ridden. Due to this, bringing your visualizations to life will help you feel more at ease.

How To Use Visualization

There are four different visualization techniques that help a person improve different areas in their life; they are; mastering new skills, healing your mind/body, achieving your goals and creating a plan.

Technique #1: Using Visualization To Master New Skills Quickly

Visualization can be used to not only learn a new skill but to master it as well. Visualization is really effective in mastering new skills because due to how the brain is exactly the same when stimulated. Someone who is visualizing the skill has the same brain activity as when they physically do that skill. Let's take a look at a study that an Australian psychologist did that studied the effectiveness of visualization regarding a person's ability to do free throws in basketball.

This psychologist chose three groups of students at random who have never tried visualization before. The first group practiced the skill of free throwing for 20 days straight. The second group only practiced free throws twice, once on the very first day and once on the last day. The third group did the same. However, the third group spent half an hour every day visualizing themselves practicing free throws. If they had "missed" in their visualized free throw, they "practiced" getting it right the next time.

On the last day of this study, the psychologist measured how the participants improved using percentages. The group that got physical practice every day improved their free throws by 24%. The second group that only practiced twice did not improve at all. However, the third group who had practiced just as much as the second group did 23% better, nearly the same as the first group. At the end of this experiment, the psychologist published a paper that was about how most effective visualization happens when the visualizer is able to see what they are doing. In other words, the ones that practiced visualizing the free-throw actually ·felt· the basketball in their hands and ·saw· it go through the hoop and have heard it ·bounce.·

You can also use visualization to improve upon any skills you want to learn. Make sure that you try to utilize all your senses when you are visualizing yourself doing this. Below are a simple five steps to how you can use visualization to do this:

1. Choose a skill that you are interested in mastering.
2. Identify what your real-world proficiency level is in this skill.
3. Visualize yourself doing this skill in as much detail as you can use all five senses.
4. Repeat this visualization for 11 days at 20 minutes per day.
5. Perform this skill physically and keep track of measuring your improvement. Continue visualizing while doing that skill in real life if you are not satisfied with the results

Technique #2: Using Visualization To Create A Detailed Plan

As entrepreneurs, it is easy to feel stressed when thinking about your business; creating a plan of action using visualization can help you relax and motivate you to take action. This technique is most effective if you use it before you go to bed so you can start planning the next day's work. However, you can use this technique throughout the day if you have 10 minutes of free time.

Below are three simple steps on how to do this:

1. Calm yourself down, and make sure you are feeling relaxed. Sit down as it will help you get some rest from whatever you were doing before.

2. Close your eyes and start to visualize which things specifically that you want to accomplish for tomorrow. Now, visualize those actions that you'd like to do in as much detail as you can and then ask yourself these questions below:

    a. How do I want to feel?
    b. How will I interact with others?
    c. What specific actions do I want to take?
    d. What do I want?
    e. What obstacles will I potentially face?
    f. How will I overcome obstacles?
    g. What do I want to achieve?

3. The reality here is that people are not able to predict all the things that might happen to

them. When events happen unexpectedly, they can often ruin any plans that have been put in place. However, good planning isn't about planning around all possible obstacles, but it is more about adapting to the obstacles that life gives you. When you keep this in mind, it is important that you affirm with yourself at the end of your session with "this or something better will come my way". By giving yourself affirmation, you are keeping your mind open to endless possibilities. This will result in you be more ready and okay with making adjustments when unexpected things happen to you.

This process is definitely not a foolproof plan. However, this visualization will help you envision possible situations that might happen. These scenarios will allow you to be able to make better decisions as you continue to work towards your goals.

Technique #3: Using Visualization To Achieve Your Goals

By using the technique of visualization for setting goals brings a lot of value, but this technique does come with one major drawback. The most popular form of visualization is goal setting. Most people have definitely used visualization pertaining to their goals at one time or another. However, this technique may not have worked for them due to one critical flaw.

This flaw is that when people are visualizing their goals, they only focus on visualizing their end goal and nothing in between. They see within their mind's a big and flashy awesome goal that's going to be rainbows and butterflies. Yes, they are experiencing this using all of their sensory, but they simply open their eyes after the visualization feeling very inspired. However, this type of motivation is extremely short-lived because the next time this person faces an obstacle, it immediately deflates their motivation.

When this happens, people feel the need to visualize their goal again in order to create more motivation. However, because nothing happens every time they visualize their goal, their motivation doesn't grow either. In fact, every time a person hits an obstacle, and they try the process of visualization again, their motivation becomes weaker every time, and they start to lose more and more energy.

The mistake that these people are making is that they are nor properly visualizing their goals. They only see the destination, but they don't understand that achieving a goal takes much more than just that. Achieving a goal is part of a journey that is full of emotional highs and lows, wins and losses, and a journey of ups and downs. Due to this, these are the things that a person would also need to include in their visualization.

When a person visualizes their end goal, it is very effective in creating that desire and hunger. However, the proper way to use visualization is to only spend 10 percent of your time visualizing the end goal and spending the rest of the visualization time thinking about HOW you will achieve your goals and overcome challenges. In some ways, it's similar to the form of visualization planning that we just discussed.

A person's end goal helps keep inspiration running in the long term, but it is the journey that helps a person stay motivated in the short term. The way to maximize the time spent on achieving small goals to get to your end goal, you must visualize those as well.

Below are five steps that you can follow to achieve this visualization:

1. Get yourself to a quiet place and sit down and close your eyes. Start to visualize your end goal. Imagine yourself experiencing and living this goal using all five of your senses.

2. Slowly take a few steps backward from your end goal and start to visualize the process that you took that lead to you achieving your end goal. Imagine all the problems, and you faced that put you back. However, you can see yourself finding solutions to those problems. Continue visualizing until you are all the way back to the present moment.

3. Now, move forward with time and visualize how you took on opportunities that helped you overcome your problems.

4. At the end of this visualization, take a few moments to send your future self some positive energy for their journey.

5. When you exit the visualization, emotionally detach from the outcome of your goal. The thing that can hold you back is if you are having an emotional attachment to a specific result. Instead, try to stay open-minded and be flexible for what's to come on your journey.

You can use visualization using those steps on a daily or weekly basis. Weekly sessions can be as long as 30 minutes and you can keep your daily sessions shorter, so they are between 5 - 10 minutes. However, be sure that you are using your daily sessions to visualize the next steps of achieving your goal for the upcoming week. This will help you continue moving forward to reach your goal. After that, you can use your weekly visualizations using the five steps above.

Strategy #2: Meditation

One of the most powerful and inspiring things that humans can do is being able to visualize the things that they want to manifest and then actually making it happen. The power of the human mind is extraordinary, especially when it is coupled with mindfulness practices like meditation. Using meditation, a person can increase their ability and make heaps of progress towards the life that they want to create for themselves. As an entrepreneur, you MUST have a vision for your business. A weak vision will not suffice in this scenario; you must have a clear and defined vision of what you want your business to be.

Goal setting is the first action that a person needs to make in order to reach their goals. The purpose behind setting a goal is so that a person would be able to achieve their desired results. When a goal is set carefully with focus, momentum, action, and intention, setting and achieving goals is the first step a person needs to take in order to move from where they are not to where they want to be. However, they need to know where it is that they want to be—the "where" begins with a person envisioning it.

The first step to this is to start with imaging the end in mind and work backward (this is what we discussed in the visualization chapter. Many people mistake their goal for vision, thinking when the goal is actually the end result. They will set a goal without thinking about what the goal will allow them to do, be, or have in the long term. In order for a person to make the most out of their goal-setting process, it is important to think about what quality of lifestyle they would want to ultimately achieve. For the purpose of clarity, let's talk a little bit more between a person's vision and their goal.

A person's vision isn't something that needs to be created from scratch; in fact, it is something that already exists inside them. They simply need to get in touch with it. A person's vision is the big picture of their desired outcomes. It represents the most important things to that person and is often compelling, inspiring, exciting, and filled with many positive emotions. A goal, on the other hand, is different. A goal is very specifically designed that requires tasks that need to be completed in order to get to the thing that they want at the end of their journey. The downside here is that a person's goal may not initiate those positive emotions that become an inspiration. Goals act more like stepping stones on a path that will lead you to your ultimate end goal.

The most popular and effective way to build your goals is using the SMART goals format. You may have done or heard of this before at your workplace or while you were in school. SMART stands for specific, measurable, achievable, resources, and time. This helps you make sure that your goals are specific and concise, you have a way of measuring them, they are goals that are achievable, you have or have a way of getting the necessary resources and you have a timeline in which you want your goals to be met.

By using imagery that is vivid and highly detailed, it is a very powerful way for someone to train their mind to go after the things that they want. Remember, when we discussed how athletes often use visualization to help themselves train? For example, famous golf athlete Tiger Woods has been using visualization to help train his golfing techniques ever since he was a teenager. Even the NBA star Michael Jordan used mental imagery to help get himself into the mindset that he wants to be in order to make his famous three-point shots. If professional athletes use visualization techniques, they can enhance their ability to be the best. You can also use visualization and meditation to help you achieve your goals.

How To Use Meditation

As an entrepreneur, you have to break down your one large goal into numerous smaller ones. This meditation guide will help you combine meditation and visualization with helping you better focus on your goals. Follow these steps:

1. Start by thinking of an area of your life in your mind. Choose something where you have been struggling with, or you would like to change.

2. Now start to imagine the best possible outcome that you would like to be living in regards to the area that you've selected. Imagine this 6 to 12 months from now. What is the reality that you are looking to achieve? Try not to get caught up with any negativity or limitations; instead, just allow yourself to imagine and get carried away with your strongest goals.

3. Focus your mind on connecting with just one goal that you would like to achieve over the next three months. Make sure your goal is a good one and is as meaningful as possible. If you choose a goal that isn't meaningful or doesn't hold a lot of weight, the end result won't feel special for you. Make sure to choose something that is significant enough so that once you achieve this goal, you will feel a high sense of accomplishment and motivation for your next goal. Be sure to run your goal through the SMART acronym to ensure that it is a goal that is set up for success.

4. Now that you are starting to feel connected with the goal that you've set, try to imagine what your life will be like once you achieve the goal. Visualize a picture or movie in your mind and try to view it as if you are looking at it through your own pair of eyes. Factor in all the other sensory perceptions to try to imagine the most real and positive feelings. Where are you? Who is with you? What are the things happening around you?

5. Now, begin to step out of the picture or movie that you've imagined and begin to imagine yourself floating up in the air above where you are sitting now while taking that imagery with you. Take a deep breath and as you breathe out, use your breath to give life to the image and fill it with intention and positive energy. Repeat this five times.

6. In this step, it is time to imagine yourself floating out into the future while imagining yourself dropping the imagery that you've created for your goal down into your real-life below you at the exact time and date that you've set for yourself to reach this goal.

7. Pay attention to all the things that need to happen between then and now and how it is beginning to re-evaluate itself in order to support you in achieving that goal. Visualize this process and all those events to make it feel as realistic as possible.

8. Once you feel like that step is complete, bring your awareness back to the present, and with your eyes still shut, start to think about what steps you will need to take in the next few days that will help you move closer to achieving your goal.

9. Take a few more deep breaths in order to ground yourself to the present before opening your eyes. Now, before you forget, write down a list of steps that you need to take in order to achieve your goal or begin to write down your experience in your journal, so you don't forget.

10. In this last step, you will focus on taking action and staying focused. Make sure that you are doing something that brings you closer to achieving your goal on a daily basis.

Use this meditation and visualization technique once a week after you first complete the steps. By doing this once a week, it helps you continue to move forward towards your end goal and help you bring your vision into real life. Seeing is believing, so using your mind and meditation, you are able to create the best future that you have imagined for yourself.

Chapter 7: How To Stop Procrastinating

As an entrepreneur, you are bound to face many obstacles throughout starting your own business. Different types of businesses will come with its own set of obstacles. Although I can't advise you on each and every single one of those problems, I can advise you on the main obstacle that entrepreneurs face – procrastination. Since starting your own business, you are technically your own boss; there is no one to hold you accountable except yourself. If you have a bad habit of procrastination in your life, this is an obstacle you MUST overcome as an entrepreneur. Otherwise, you will end up with a lackluster business. In this chapter, I will be teaching you about how procrastination works, how you can overcome it, and I will teach you to break out of your excuses. If you can overcome this bad habit, then I guarantee that you will have your business up and running in no time.

Procrastination Is An Entrepreneur's Biggest Enemy

So why is procrastination an entrepreneur's biggest enemy? Let's learn more about the science behind this. Through an abundance of psychology research, psychologists have discovered a phenomenon called "time inconsistency," which helps explain why procrastination affects humans so largely by pulling us away from needed tasks despite our good intentions. The term time inconsistency refers to the habit of the human mind to value immediate gratification or rewards more highly compared to long-term and future rewards. The best way to further understand this is to imagine that you have two alter egos. The first is your present self, and the second is your future self. When a person sets goals for themselves, such as getting fit by working out more or learning a new language, they are actually making plans for their future self. They are envisioning what they want their life to be like in the future. Evidence has shown researchers that when a person thinks about their future self, it is not difficult for their brain to see the value of doing actions that will lead to long-term benefits. The future self is the one that values long-term rewards.

On the contrary, while the future self can only set goals, the present self is the one that is responsible for taking action. There will come a time where this individual will need to make a decision, but they aren't making a choice for the future self at this point. In the present moment, their brain is focused entirely on the present self. Research shows that the present self prefers immediate rewards over long-term ones. This means that the present self and future self don't often get along. While the future self wants to be healthy and have a sic pack, the present self wants some chili cheese fries. Everyone knows that eating unhealthy will prevent health problems in the future when you're at an old age, but those things are so far away, so why worry about them now right? This is the thought process that many people have when they are faced with a choice of immediate gratification or achieving long-term goals.

Very similarly, most young people know that saving money for their retirement during their 20s and 30s is extremely valuable, but the benefit of this is many decades away. It is much easier for a person's present-self to see value in buying themselves a new iPhone rather than putting away $1000 for their 75-year-old self! This concept of "time inconsistency" may be the reason why people often go to bed feeling motivated and inspired to reach their goals and change their life but they find themselves completely falling back into bad habits when they wake up. This is due to the fact that the human brain values long-term benefits when they are thinking about the future, but it prefers immediate gratification when it comes to the present moment. Let's dive into a little bit more of the science behind this.

For the sake of example here, let's pretend for a little while that you are a giraffe living in the plains of the African savanna. Your neck is 6 feet long, and occasionally, you will see a group of human tourists driving in a car with a safari tour taking pictures of you. However, it's not just your long neck that separates you from the humans. It could be that the biggest difference between you and your other giraffe friends and the humans taking pictures is that almost every single decision that you make brings an immediate benefit to your life. For example, when you see a storm coming, you will find shelter under a tree, or if you are hungry, you walk over to the nearest tree and begin to eat, or when you spot a predator hunting you, you begin to run away.

Every day, most of the choices that you make as a giraffe, such as where to sleep when to avoid a predator, or what to eat, make a direct and immediate impact on your life. You are entirely focused on the present, and the furthest you would think about in the near future. You are living in an ·Immediate-Return Environment·; this is what scientists call this environment due to the fact that your actions deliver very immediate and clear outcomes.

Now let's change things up and pretend that you are one of the human tourists that are traveling in Africa on the safari. Different from giraffes, humans live in a ·Delayed Return Environment.· Most of the choices made in this type of environment will not benefit you right away. For example, if you save your money now, you'll have enough for retirement in forty years, or if you work hard at your job today, you will get paid in two weeks. Rewards are designed to be delayed until some point in the future in many aspects of modern-day society.

While the giraffe is worried about problems that are immediate, such as avoiding predators, seeking shelters, and finding food, humans worry the most about the problems of the future. For instance, while the humans are on the safari, they may be thinking, ·This trip and safari has been tremendous fun! It would be so awesome if I could work as a safari tour guide and be able to see the giraffes every day. Speaking of work, is it time for me to change my career? Am I really working the kind of job that I enjoy? Should I start looking for new jobs?·

Unfortunately for us, humans that are living in a Delayed Return Environment tend to lead to a lot of anxiety and stress. This is because the human brain wasn't designed to solve problems of a Delayed Return Environment. In fact, this is why there has been a rise in depression and anxiety over the last decade. Where people of the past focused more on their immediate problem like harvesting their crops for food or boiling water, so it's safe to drink, people nowadays focus on problems that are in the future since most of our basic needs are already taken care of.

Why Are Entrepreneur's Prone To Procrastination?

There are many reasons as to why an entrepreneur would choose to procrastinate rather than to work on their largest goal. Procrastination is probably one of the biggest obstacles that hinder a person from being able to achieve greater things. Everyone has procrastinated before, and anyone is capable of it. Many times, people don't even know that they are procrastinating. However, there are also those moments where people know that they are procrastinating but fail to do anything to stop the process. So why do people procrastinate anyways, although they are self-aware? There are numerous reasons why people begin procrastinating; let's take a look at the most common ones:

Skill insufficiency

An entrepreneur needs to develop new skills and improve on existing ones in order to build a successful business. That's a non-negotiable. However, people often fail to see this fact. They see their lack of skill or knowledge as an obstacle that is permanent and cannot be overcome. This mindset causes people to give up on their goals before they have even done anything to start it. Rather than giving up, people need to be able to assess the skills and knowledge that are required to achieve their goal and then compare it to their own skills and knowledge that they possess. The difference between the two is nothing more than just an opportunity to learn and train. Instead of just giving up, people need to create a plan that will help them develop and learn the skills needed in order to bridge that gap. So is it procrastination if you are pushing the date of your goal achievement back? Absolutely not. This is just effective planning. By understanding that you require more time to reach your goal means that you are identifying the right steps, you need to take to reach your goal.

Fear of success

Many professionals of the self-help industry have talked or theorized about the fact that people's biggest fear wasn't necessarily a failure, but our biggest fear is actually the fear of success. Many people view success as stress and pressure. When they think about achieving greater and more things, they often think about the negative aspects that come with it. For example, they believe that when a person achieves more, people will begin to demand and expect more from you. They often doubt their ability to deal with the increased expectations, so they decide to procrastinate to sabotage their own chances of success. As an entrepreneur, you need to relish in the thought of success, not be afraid of it

As a person begins to succeed by overcoming the challenges of all difficulties, they begin to become more knowledgeable and have developed new skills. Their resilience will begin to increase. If a person is able to learn the necessary skills of personal organization, it really doesn't matter what type of task or work that they are doing, they will be able to find a way through. Long story short, every task is simply just a task that needs to be completed. When you are able to break down every large task into a number of smaller tasks, there should be nothing that would be able to overwhelm you.

Fear of failure

There are a lot of people who have the belief that failure is devastating. They often see failure as a final result that is set in stone and cannot be rectified or changed. Failure to them is a permanent stain on their reputation, which means that every time that they fail, their ego takes a huge hit. This lack of confidence causes them to avoid taking action on tasks where they are not 100% absolutely confident in its success. Keep in mind that in the era that we live in today, many tasks that people face will be new to them and it is entirely impossible to be able to be 100% confident in every single chance of success. Due to this, procrastination is something that happens frequently and in an endless spiral.

On the contrary, there are the people out there who see failure as a stepping stone towards success and a learning opportunity. They have the understanding and belief that mistakes are unavoidable, and they will be made. Their attitude consists mostly of realistic optimism, which enables them to believe that they will be able to successfully achieve their goal/task even if it's something that requires more than one try. As you might be able to tell, these types of people have a much lower tendency to procrastinate. Instead, they often approach new challenges with excitement and preparedness to deal with obstacles.

Since learning and growth are important parts of a successful life, it is unrealistic to believe that you can succeed without experiencing any obstacles or failures in your journey. If you are constantly worrying and are scared at the idea of failure, try to identify extra steps or measures that you can take in order to lower the chances of failure and increase the chances of success. Factor in time that you can take to review and assess your own actions and try to learn something from every experience. You will soon start to change your mindset into one where you see every challenge as an opportunity for learning and growth.

Lack of interest

Everyone has their own special set of interests. Just because your friend is passionate about a particular topic or job, it does not mean that everyone else is interested in the same thing. People have the tendency to put off doing jobs that they do not find interesting because it is more difficult to find motivation. There are multiple ways that people can deal with jobs that they have no interest in depending on if you are the person that is actually doing the job or if they are the person that is simply assigning the task. Let's take a look at the perspective of a person that is physically doing the job; they could try the following things:

- Check to see if this task actually has to be done
- Ask yourself if there is someone else who is much better suited to completing this task. If possible, you may be able to swap it or delegate it (e.g., if someone else likes that job better, you can trade with them for the one that you might like better)
- If your tolerance for frustration is low, try to break down this job into smaller pieces and complete them one at a time
- If your tolerance for frustration is higher, you can schedule a block of time where you take away all distractions and just do this task until it is done

From the perspective of the person who is assigning the job/task, you will likely find more success if you assign this specific task to someone who you know will be passionate about it. By choosing someone who has an interest in that task, the job will be completed in a much faster fashion and at a higher standard as well.

Lack of motivation

Entrepreneurs often have the wrong mindset where they think that they need to feel fully motivated before they start working on a task/job. This mindset is unrealistic. People's motivation often does not arrive until they have started that task and is beginning to see progress. When people see progress, they start to see the fruits to their labor and they become even more motivated to keep working until they have completed their task. You might be wondering what about the motivation that is needed in order to start working altogether? The answer to this is that a person needs to have a good understanding of the 'why' and the vision of that particular job. Before you even begin working on it, you should know what the benefits are going to be. You would be surprised at how many people waste a lot of time doing work that actually does not need to be completed. Moreover, people should be using prioritization in order to get the most urgent and important work out of the way first. By understanding the benefits of completing a task or job, you will fully be able to estimate its importance. In terms of smaller tasks/jobs, simply understanding what the benefits are of completing that task should be enough for motivation. For larger tasks and jobs, it is important that you have a way to measure your progress so you can further gain motivation and confidence from your work.

Resistance

You might have experienced this phenomenon before, where there are times that it would be easier for you to just complete a task than procrastinate but yet you still chose to procrastinate! The main reason for this is rebellion. There is a class of procrastinators called the 'rebellious procrastinators'; they are very common. These people deliberately delay tasks, defy standards, falter expectations, and impedes protocol. This type of procrastination can be done by anyone, especially if they feel like they have been mistreated.

The reasons that cause people to procrastinate are different for every individual. The exact reason why each individual may not be obvious, but the obvious reasons may be caused by something that is underlying. On the contrary, the reasons that we had just discussed are seen as the most common ones. Trying to avoid this type of behavior is not an easy task as it often involves a person to identify their bad habits and actively try to break them down and create new ones. Whether you are the procrastinator or you are suffering at the hands of one, the important part here is to take action immediately. You have to take action in order to correct your situation. Keep in mind that procrastination is a serious issue that if left unresolved for a long time, can cause some serious and long-lasting problems in your life.

The Vicious Cycle Of Procrastination

Procrastination arises from some of our own unhelpful rules and assumptions that we have of ourselves and the rest of the world. When these rules and assumptions are activated, they lead people to detect some sort of discomfort about doing a task or job that they've set up for themselves in the past. If the person is unable to tolerate this discomfort, they will likely utilize procrastination as a method of avoiding this discomfort. They often can come up with pretty convincing justifications or excuses for their procrastination, but they will be more likely to go down the route of procrastinating. Due to this, they will end up engaging in procrastination activities such as instant gratification things that create a pleasurable distraction that substitutes the task that they are supposed to be doing. In return, there are consequences that come up due to this procrastination, which will make the person more likely to go down the route of procrastination again the next time they are faced with a similar task or job. This cycle happens because people got a ·reward· or pay-off for their procrastination, and they have made that task even more aversive by avoiding it in the first place.

To help give you a visualization of this cycle, here is a little chart that will help explain it further.

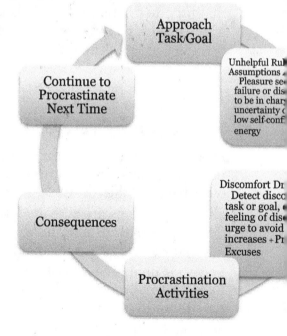

How To Overcome Procrastination So You Can Build A Successful Business

With your new understanding of procrastination and the causes behind it, it's time to get hands-on and learn how to overcome it. I have mapped out a 10-step guide for you to follow to help you overcome the biggest challenge with entrepreneurs.

1. Break down your business goals into smaller tasks.

We learned that entrepreneurs typically have a bad habit of procrastinating their work because they are overwhelmed. Start by just breaking down whatever that task is into littler parts and then focus on one at a time. If you find yourself still wanting to procrastinate after you've already broken it down, then break it down even more. You will eventually get to a point where the task that you need to do is so easy that you would feel very badly about yourself if you didn't just do it.

Let's use an example regarding filing taxes. As an entrepreneur, one important task that you have to do is to properly file your business taxes at the end of the year. Imagine that you are feeling overwhelmed as you don't even know where to begin when filing your taxes. You are also afraid that you may owe money to the government that you might not have. Here is how I would break down the large and broad task of ·filing taxes':

1. Research the best way to file taxes for entrepreneurs
2. Explore my options (either downloading software for DIY or going to a tax filing company)
3. Pick which option suits you best
4. Gather the documents that are suggested based on which option you chose in step #2
5. Follow the instructions given to you by the tax software or the tax professional

Suddenly that one large task of 'filing taxes' became much more manageable. Instead of thinking about filing taxes as one large unit, you are now starting with a simple google search of the best way to file taxes for beginners. From there, now you can make an educated decision on which method is easiest for you to proceed with. By taking things one step at a time, your mind becomes less overwhelmed.

2. Change your working/business environment. This may be obvious to some, but different types of environments produce different impacts on a person's productivity. Take a look at your workspace, does looking at it make you want to go back to bed? Or does it look inviting enough to make you want to jump right into work? If it's the former, you may want to consider changing up your workspace to make it more inviting. For instance, I used to have stronger feelings of procrastination when my desk was cluttered. It did not look inviting, and in fact, it added stress as now I needed to clear up my workspace before doing a task that I didn't even really want to do in the first place. By keeping your workspace clean,

tidy, and inviting, you can skip the step of having to tidy up before getting your hands dirty with work.

3. Create a detailed business plan (include deadlines).

When a person just has one singular deadline for a large task, it's basically an invitation to procrastinate. This is because people get under the impression that they have time and continue to keep pushing things back until the deadline is looming over them. In step one, we discussed breaking down your task into smaller ones. In this step, we will actually make our own deadlines for each small task. The purpose of this is, so you have a general idea when you have to finish each task. If you don't finish one step by the deadline that you have set, you are jeopardizing every step that's planned after that. This helps create some urgency.

4. Get rid of all your temptations.

If you are someone who is a constant procrastination offender, it may be because you make it very easy for yourself to be distracted. Be self-aware – what are the things that you typically find yourself doing when you're supposed to be doing something else? Is it browsing the internet? Scrolling your phone? Identify what exactly it is that is tempting you to procrastinate and try to prevent yourself from being tempted in the first place. If you are easily distracted by your phone, turn it off for an hour, put it in a drawer, and begin to work. Some people may extreme and go as far as disabling all their social media accounts so they can prevent themselves from endless browsing. It doesn't have to be extremely drastic but take preventative measures, so it's not too easy for you to procrastinate.

5. Be in the company of people who inspire you. Choosing who you spend your time with heavily influences your behaviors. If you are spending time with people who also procrastinate and don't see anything wrong with it, then you are likely to think that that is okay. Instead, try to surround yourself with people that are motivated and have achieved many goals before. You will soon be able to gain some of their motivation and spirit as well.

6. Find an entrepreneur, buddy. When you have a large set of tasks that you need to get done, having a buddy will make the process way more fun, your buddy should ideally be someone that also has their own large set of tasks/goals that they want to complete. The two of you will hold each other accountable for the tasks that need to be done. It is not required that both of you need to have the same goals, but if they are, even better! Many people that have goals of getting more fit will likely find themselves a workout buddy that will help hold them accountable for going to the gym or even planning workout sessions together.

7. Let others in on your goals. This serves a similar function as the step before but on a much larger scale. Tell your friends, family, and colleagues about the goals that you have in mind. This works better if you tell them details like your deadlines or the plan that you've made for yourself.

Now the next time you see these people, they will
likely ask you what your status is on your goals,
therefore, creating motivation for you. Also, people
tend to not want to ·fail· in front of others, so if you
know that you are seeing those people soon, you are
more likely to make sure that you have made some
progress so you can update them on it.

8. Network with successful entrepreneurs.
If your goal is one that you think other people have
accomplished before, try to find out who these people
are. Seek them out and connect with them in order to
ask them about their experience. You can learn about
what obstacles and failures that they faced along the
way, and they'd be able to provide you with some tips
that may have made their journey a little bit easier.
Moreover, seeing living proof that your goals are ones
that are achievable may help you take action even
sooner.

9. Re-assess your goals consistently.
If you are someone that has been procrastinating for a
long time now, it might be due to the misalignment of
what you're currently doing and what you want.
People often outgrow their goals when they begin to
learn more about themselves. However, they don't
always adjust their goals based on those changes. Try
to take a weekend to yourself and regroup. Ask
yourself, ·what exactly do I want to achieve? Are the
things that I am doing now aligning with that? If not,
what can I do to change it?· Adjusting your goals to
something that lines up with who you are presently is

crucial in terms of creating motivation and value for yourself.

10. Don't overcomplicate your business plan. This relates back to a point we talked about earlier in this book. There is never a ·perfect time· to do a task that you need to do. You may be identifying all the reasons why the present moment is ·not the best time,· but that is the wrong mindset to have. Even if you only had 10 minutes, you can surely get SOMETHING done that is related to your goal. Abandon this thought of waiting for ·the perfect time· because there will never be one. After you break down your goals into smaller ones, start doing them whenever you have 10 minutes free. It's as simple as that.

Breaking Free From Your Procrastination Excuses

Overcoming your procrastination excuses is an important step in fighting procrastination altogether. Understanding common excuses that entrepreneurs use will help you better prepare yourself for when those excuses arise. When you are able to break free from your procrastination excuses, you can actually get started on the tasks that are important to you. In this chapter, I will be teaching you about the most common excuses that entrepreneurs use. I will also provide you with some tips to help you break free from these excuses. Let's take a look at the following excuses.

- "I don't have time to do this right now."
Entrepreneurs who rely on this excuse the most are usually busy professionals that are also working a full-time job. They never feel like they are using an excuse because it is true that they are actually always busy. If someone is constantly on the go and completing tasks but still never getting to the end of their to-do list, it may feel natural to think that you don't have time for whatever task you promised yourself you would do. However, there is a huge flaw in this type of mindset. There will always be time to work on something; you just have to make room for it. We talked about how you can do a lot in 10 minutes of time. Simply just set aside 10 minutes of time in the morning or right before bed. That is really all you need. You'll then start to make gradual progress without the need to interfere with your daily schedule.

- "I'll do this tomorrow."
This excuse usually appears during a person's childhood. However, a large number of adults use this excuse on a daily basis. There is an old saying that goes "never put off till tomorrow what you can do today." Unfortunately, this saying does not stand up well in the face of the temptation of instant gratification. Instead of resisting temptation, try to think of it in a way where you're doing yourself a favor. Promise yourself some type of reward (e.g., getting your favorite take out or drawing yourself a nice bath) if you do that required task today instead of tomorrow.

- "This task is too hard to do right now."

People that set themselves up for large tasks without making a plan often fall victim to this excuse. When a person looks at a huge set of tasks, all they can see is how big and overwhelming that one entity is. When all you're thinking about is how big that workload is, it's almost natural that you would want to avoid it for as long as possible. Rather than looking at your one large task as a monstrous unit, break it down into smaller chunks. We already talked about this, but by breaking down your task into smaller ones and focusing on those smaller ones individually, you are giving yourself an in that feels much less intimidating.

- "I'll start working on Y once I finish X."

When a person has two competing tasks or goals, inevitably, one will take a backseat. It is important to have more than one priority, but dividing your attention entirely is not the ideal way to confront this. For instance, let's say that you are working on two projects that have the same deadline at the end of the week. By the end of your first day working, you've already made a huge impact on project A but you don't want to start project B because you don't want to shift gears. In order to not make the excuse to put off project B, start doing some preliminary tasks that project B requires in the background. You can take short 5 minute breaks from project A just to make a plan for project B. This way, when you complete project A, you already have a whole plan mapped out for project B, and you can get your feet wet right away without losing momentum.

- "This task isn't important enough to do right now."

This excuse comes in multiple forms. The first form of it is that you believe that this task should not even be your responsibility in the first place. For instance, your manager could have given you a task that generally isn't your responsibility. In this scenario, you may be procrastinating because you resent the fact that you got extra work. If there is an opening for you to negotiate with your boss about this task, then, by all means, go for it. However, if you know that there is no getting out of it, you might as well start sooner rather than later. Secondly, a task that you deem not important enough maybe something that is of a preventative or routine measure. These tasks tend to take a backseat in comparison to more urgent tasks, but they are also often swept under the rug when a person thinks they are insignificant. If you find yourself thinking that certain tasks just 'aren't important enough,' remind yourself that routine upkeep tasks prevent large problems in the future. If we use dental cleaning as an example, it's a lot cheaper to just get your routine check-up and cleaning every year rather than putting it off and having to do costly dental work when something does happen to you.

- "This task is too important; I need to do it with my full attention."

The most common victims to fall into this excuse are your nervous professionals. For instance, let's pretend that there is a huge project that's been neglected for a while but there are a ton of your daily tasks that you still need to complete. If you truly believe that your project is the most important thing right now, you may decide to do it at a time where you aren't distracted by other trivial tasks. It does sort of make sense on one hand when it comes to a person doing their best work when they have minimal distractions. However, there will never be a time where there are no distractions. People will always have interference, and just like what we learned earlier, there is no 'perfect' time to do something. Rather than saying now is not the best time to work on it, break it down into smaller tasks and just do one of them amidst your other tasks.

- "I'm too stressed (or tired, angry, sad...etc.) to do this right now."

This excuse is probably the most used, common, and tempting one of them all. If a person finds themselves in a negative mood, all they want to do is to stop working and do something that will make them feel better. This could be just sitting at home relaxing or going out for a beer. This results in the person rationalizing with themselves that their work would be done faster and with more productivity if they try to attempt it when they are feeling better. There are two important aspects to note here. First of all, it is impossible to tell what kind of mood someone will be in the future. For all we know, this person could be in the same exact mood tomorrow and fall into the same excuse, like some sort of unproductive loop. Secondly, this is not a common thought but working through a hard task can actually enhance someone's mood. The feeling of achievement and satisfaction that comes with finishing a task, no matter how pleasant or unpleasant, often lifts people out of a bad mood. Especially if they can get a reward after that, they feel like they deserved it.

Now that you know what the most common excuses are, which ones do you feel like you use most often? When you know which excuses you use most frequently, you can begin to test them to see if these excuses have any truth in them. For example, I am a constant offender of using the "I'm too tired" excuse. Although it is true that I am often tired due to long hours of writing, I need to test my excuse of whether or not I am too tired to do a required task that I need to do. In this scenario, I would ask myself, "Am I really too tired to write one more chapter?" and then "Am I too tired to watch TV or scroll on social media?" Almost nine times out of ten, my answer is no, I am not too tired to watch TV or browse the web. Therefore, my excuse for "I'm too tired" is a lie and I do have the energy to do some work.

Try testing your most common excuses by asking yourself these questions below, based on which excuse you find yourself using.

Your Excuse	Questions To Ask Y To Test Said Excus
"I will do it tomorrow."	<ul><li>What is my sch tomorrow?</li><li>Do I actually h. tomorrow?</li></ul>

	• What are t do this task have any re
"I don't have enough time to do this right now."	• How much have at leas time) • What smal short amou
"This is too hard to do right now."	• Why is it t the tasks it break down ones) • Will this ta tomorrow? matter of ti breaking yo • What will r do right no
"Once I finish X, I'll start working on Y."	• Is there no finishing X make my ta • Can I at lea Y? • What is the able to sim done X? (If start some finished tas
"This task is too important; it requires my full attention."	• Is there goi where my a undivided? good as any

"It's not important enough."	• What else is mo[re important] now? • Why do I think [it's not] important enou[gh]? • If I neglect this [will it come] up to me later? [or do I need to do] it right now)
"I'm too tired (or stressed, sad, angry...etc.)"	• Am I going to b[e feeling] other negative e[motions] • How will I know [when I] will be feeling b[etter] • Can anyone kno[w how I am] going to be feeli[ng]

Chapter 8: How To Become A Competent Money Manager

At this point in the book, we have covered all the important traits you need to have in terms of mindset. We can now move on to the second part of this book, where we will learn more about financial skills that will help you become a successful entrepreneur. To do this, we will start off simply by learning about money management and what some good characteristics are. This will act as your guideline so you don't stray too far away from your finances. Then, I will teach you the basics of money management by teaching you how to analyze income statements, balance sheets, and cash flows. Let's get started.

Characteristics Of A Competent Money Manager

Competent money managers always share the same three characteristics. Firstly, they never spend beyond their means, ever. Even if there was a significant opportunity, they would never take out more money than they need to invest in it. Secondly, they always have a good stash of emergency savings. This is where they have money saved up for a rainy day, so they don't have to go into debt or bankruptcy. Thirdly, competent money managers assess their risks before taking one. This does not mean they don't take any risks at all because as an entrepreneur, you have to take risks. However, they take calculated risks. Let's cover the first characteristic first.

1. Competent money managers will never spend beyond their means

Competent money managers will never spend more than what they already have. What does this mean? This means that they will never spend more money than they have in their immediate accounts. Most competent money managers will have some savings reserved for emergency purposes. That stash of money does not get touched unless it is for emergencies. They also will never take out a loan or pay for things with a credit card if they don't already have that existing money in their debit accounts. Not spending beyond your means will prevent you from getting yourself into debt. Moreover, most people that spend beyond their means usually spend their money on things that are non-essential. They may be tempted to buy a new car as a big sale at a local dealership is temping them due to low monthly rates. Competent money managers will not spend their money on a new car unless it is utterly essential for their living and that they are 100% sure they can pay off the car without needing to sign up for ridiculously high-interest rates or long financing terms. Let me explain this more with an example. Let's use an entrepreneur named John. John is starting out his own café. He is in the process of getting the equipment and space ready to build his shop. His income after all business and living expenses comes to about $1000 per month. One of his friends convinces him that as a new business owner, he should look the part and therefore, advises him to buy a fancy suit. This suit costs $1500. If John is a competent money manager, this purchase is absolutely beyond his means. If he purchases this

$1500 suit, it would mean that he has to spend the remaining monthly income he has and likely has to dip into his savings or put the overage of $500 on a credit card. In a situation like John's, a competent money manager would never make this purchase. Instead, they would likely go with one of two options. You can either purchase a cheaper suit that IS within your means, approximately $200 - $300 will be fine. Or, you could set aside $200 - $300 every month for 4 - 5 months until you have saved the money to comfortably afford this suit without having to compromise your business or everyday living. As an entrepreneur, your money is your investment. Choosing to not spend it on things that are beyond your affordability will ensure that you are spending your money to get the highest return.

2. Competent money managers always have emergency savings

Emergencies happen to everyone. It can come in the form of a flooded basement or a large medical bill. Competent money managers are people that avoid living paycheck to paycheck. Instead, they make an effort to save at least 10% of their income every month into their emergency savings. The purpose of emergency savings is to prevent unforeseen circumstances from bankrupting you. Those who live paycheck to paycheck without any sort of emergency savings can be thrown into financial turmoil if they are suddenly stuck with a $5,000 medical bill. Let's use another example to explain why a competent money manager always has emergency savings.

Imagine that Holly is an entrepreneur who has just started her own business consulting business. Business is steady, but she's not making as much money as she would like. She has been running her business as her full-time job and makes about $4000 per month. Her living expenses and business expenses come up to about $2000 per month, which means she has $2000 left over. As a competent money manager, Holly makes sure that she saves at least $1000 per month with a goal of a total of $10,000 for her emergency savings. Currently, she has about $3000 saved up. Unfortunately, Holly's dog suddenly fell ill and had to go through major surgery. The veterinarian quoted her $2,500 for the surgery. Luckily, Holly already has $3,000 saved up to spend on emergencies, so this sudden surgery will not affect her largely. Now, if Holly weren't a competent money manager and didn't have ANY emergency savings along with spending beyond her means, this would mean that Holly would have no money to pay for the surgery. Instead, she would likely have to take out a loan or rely on a credit card to pay for her dog's surgery. In this example, you can see why having emergency savings will prevent you from needing to go into debt if something were to happen. As an entrepreneur, there are risks that come with running a business and just everyday life in general. As a rule of thumb, aim to have $10,000 of emergency savings that you can dip into if an expensive accident happens. This will prevent you from needing to stress or needing to take out a high-interest loan to pay for the emergency.

3. Competent money managers take calculated risks

Competent money managers only take calculated risks. You often hear of people purchasing and selling stocks to make a lot of money quickly. Although this does work, there is a ton of risk involved. Competent money managers usually would not take risks such as purchasing stock as there is no guaranteed return. Instead, they usually use their money to invest in other financial products that have less risk. For instance, a common investment that competent money managers like to invest in is real estate. Although you require quite an initial heft sum of money, the return on it is usually quite high. Here is an example. Kate has savings of $30,000 and is looking for an investment. She is deciding between investing her $30,000 into several different types of stocks or using her $30,000 as a down payment for a house. If Kate were a competent money manager, the choice she would make would be to invest $30,000 in a house as long as the real estate in her market is steady. Usually, house prices increase by 5% - 10% every year, which guarantees her an investment return of 5% - 10%. If she chooses to invest her $30,000 into stocks, she is putting her money at a lot of risks as stocks can drop in price in a matter of days while the housing market typically takes longer to drop, and you are provided with much more notice. Simply just by looking at these two options, a competent money manager will see that investing in real-estate is the safer choice with high returns. If you are just starting out in managing your money, don't dabble with stocks unless you have knowledge and experience first.

How To Read And Analyze Basic Financial Statements

In this subchapter, I will be teaching you how to read and analyze your basic financial statements. These statements are usually; income statements, balance sheets, and cash flows. If you are someone who has gone to business school or taking finance/accounting at a college or university level, you probably already know this information. If not, you will want to pay extra attention. Let's start by learning income statements first.

Income Statements

An income statement is a bare minimum that you would need to know in order for you to manage the finances of your business. The purpose of an income statement is simple; it tells you whether you are profiting or losing money. Here is an example of a very simple income statement of a child's allowance:

Revenue or Gross Income: $5.00
Expenses: $2.00 (Candy)
Net Income: $3.00

See how simple this is? The first line is the money that is coming into your possession, while the second line is the money going out of your possession. The bottom line is the difference between the two. Since the number is positive, it means you are making money. If the net income is negative, it means you are losing money. Income statements can be as simple as such, but it does get more complicated the larger your company gets.

As companies grow larger and larger, they include a few more variations of the same structure. For instance, they may have additional lines such as; "cost of revenue" or "gross profit." They may also have additional lines differentiating their income such as; "operating income" or "income before taxes." Entrepreneurs need to ensure that their income statements are accurate because they need to see whether their business is succeeding or not. An inaccurate income statement can cause you to think that your business is making more than it actually is (bad scenario) or it's making less than you think it is (better scenario). Here are a few things you can do to better analyze your income statement:

1. Double-check all the math

Errors occur in income statements, even in the biggest corporations. Finding errors can help you discover things that may change your entire business result. Check all the adding and subtracting of your revenue and costs to make sure that your numbers are accurate.

2. Look at the bottom line

One of the most basic things that you can do if you are unfamiliar with income statements is to look at the bottom line. If that number is positive, it is likely a good sign. This meant that your company has earned more money than it spent during a certain period. What this really means is that your company is able to buy equipment/materials, pay its people, taxes, and keep its lights on without needing to borrow any money. However, if that bottom number is negative, printed in red, or closed in parentheses, it means that you spend more money than you've made. Keep in mind that just because that number is negative, it does not mean that your company is failing. Often, new companies like startups typically have high start-up costs and do not make a profit until the first 1 - 3 years. However, if your losses become a trend or your company isn't one that has high costs, then you need to review your business model or you may have a big problem.

3. Look at your income sources

Looking at where your income is coming from is crucial as you want to make sure that the source is sustainable. For instance, if your business is a restaurant, then sales that come from your F&B will make sense and is sustainable - as that is the main service and product that you sell. However, if your income is mostly coming from events that don't happen regularly, then it may not be sustainable for your business. What if Christmas is over and there aren't any large holiday parties until next year? That won't be reliable in the long run. Ensure that your sales income is coming from repeatable sources and not a one-off.

4. Assess your expense categories

Make sure your expense categories make sense. In a typical business, their categories will usually be supplies, rent, insurance, wages, and interest. If there is something missing, find out why, as that could be a documentation error causing an inflated net income number.

5. Assess your biggest expenses

Depending on what your business is, your largest expense will vary. If you are a service business, then your largest expense may be in wages and salaries. If you are a manufacturing business, then your supplies and equipment may be your largest expense. If you run a massage parlor as your business and you see that your supplies and equipment expenses are larger than your wages, then something could be wrong as that doesn't make sense. Ensure that your biggest expense makes sense to avoid spending money on unnecessary things.

Balance Sheets

The balance sheet is simple to understand. Its purpose simply is to tell you more about the health of your business. There are three main numbers you should care about in a balance sheet; assets, liabilities, and shareholder's equity. Equity is simply the difference between assets and liabilities. If you have more liabilities than assets, it means that your company is at a deficit. If you have more assets than liabilities, then your company is at a surplus. Let's take a look at assets first. Companies typically have current assets and non-current assets. Current assets are items of value that your business owns that will be converted into cash within one year. A company's current assets include their; accounts receivable, inventory, and cash. The accounts receivable are short-term payments that are owed to your business. The simplest example would be the outstanding invoices that your clients will pay shortly. Inventory is for businesses that sell physical products such as electronics, clothing, furniture, ...etc. Cash can include hard currency, checks, and unrestricted bank accounts. Secondly, you will need to take a look at your non-current assets. These are assets that can't be converted to cash as easily or within one year. This can be both tangible and intangible assets. Tangible assets are physical things such as equipment, machinery, or property. Intangible assets are non-physical things such as patents, copyrights, and goodwill. Non-current assets are usually calculated with depreciation factored in which is the cost of the asset over its lifespan. Thirdly, we have our liabilities. Liabilities are a company's financial obligations that are owed to someone else. There are two types of this as well; current liabilities and long-term liabilities. Current liabilities are short-term liabilities that need to be paid within one year; this includes; payments towards long-term debts, payroll, and accounts payable. Long-term liabilities are financial obligations that are due in more than one year's time; this includes; loans and debts. Lastly, there is your shareholder's equity. Shareholder's equity means your business's total net worth. This includes the initial sum of money that the owner invested in the company. If you decide to invest your first year's net earnings into your business, you will report those numbers under shareholder's equity.

Your balance sheets are typically divided into two sides. A balance sheet is correct when both sides are equal to each other. The two sides on a balance sheet are your assets and financial obligations. The main formula of this sheet is Assets = Liabilities + Shareholders Equity.

Here is a simple example of a balance sheet from a printing company.

Assets
- Current Assets:
    - Bank Account: $3470.00
    - Petty Cash: 50.00
    - *Total Current Assets: $3520.00*
- Fixed Assets:
    - Vehicle: $4500.00
    - Printer: 1800.00
    - *Total Fixed Assets: $6300.00*
- Inventory:
    - Stock: $1500.00
- Total Assets: $11,320.00

Liabilities
- Current Liabilities:
    - Accounts Payable: $1800.00
    - *Total Current Liabilities: $1800.00*
- Long Term Liabilities
    - Vehicle Loan: $4500.00
    - *Total Long Term Liabilities: $4500.00*
- Total Liabilities: $6300.00

Equity
- Initial Investment: $5000.00
- Drawings: -$130.00
- Current Earnings: $150.00
- Total Equity: $5020.00

Following the balance sheet equation: Assets = Liabilities + Shareholders Equity, our equation would look like this:

Assets = $6300.00 + $5020.00
$11,320.00 = $11,320.00

Therefore, our balance sheet is correct.

Cash Flows

The cash flow statement is crucial in all businesses as it shows us how the company is spending its money and where their money is coming from. The cash flow statement will show you everything from all the cash it is receiving from its operations and all the cash that is leaving to pay for business costs and investments.

A cash flow statement will have three distinct sections; operations, investing, and financing. Generally, the rule of thumb is that if your business generates positive net cash flow from your operating activities, then you are doing well. If you are failing to generate positive cash flow from operating activities, then you may need to look for outside financing to keep your business operating. Ideally, you don't have to do this as it is not sustainable for a business long term.

Here is how a typical cash flow statement will look like:

Cash Flow From Operations

This section of the cash flow statement shows us how much cash is coming from the income statement. A few items under this section are accounts receivables, payables, and income taxes payable. If a client pays their invoice, it will be completed as a receivable transaction, which means it will be recorded under operations. Any changes in a company's current assets or liabilities are also recorded as cash flow from operations.

Cash Flow From Investing

This section records the cash flows that come from sales and purchases of long-term investments (fixed assets) such as equipment and property. Examples of this would be purchases of land, furniture, vehicles, or buildings. Usually, investing transactions will generate cash outflows such as expenditures for equipment, property, plant, business acquisitions, or the purchase of investment securities. Cash inflows will come from the sales of these assets.

Cash Flow From Financing

Debt and equity transactions are reported in this section. Any type of cash flows that include the repurchase/sale of bonds and stocks and payment of dividends are considered cash flows for financing activities. Cash that you receive from a loan or cash that you use to pay off a loan is also recorded in this section.

Here is a sample cash flow:

Harry's Bistro
May 2020

Cash Flows From Operating Activities
- Net Income: $98,285.71
- Receipts From Customers: $76,082.77
- Payments to employees and suppliers: -$32,846.13
- Total adjustments to reconcile net income to net cash provided by operations: $43,236.44
- *Total cash flows from operating activities: $141,522.35*

Cash Flows From Investing Activities
- Computer Equipment: -$1283.49
- Other cash items from investing activities: $2464.84
- *Total cash flows from investing activities: $1181.35*

Cash Flows Financing Activities
- Other cash items from financing activities: $5000.00
- *Total cash flows from financing activities: $5000.00*

Net cash increase for period: $147,703.70

Cash Balances:

- Net cash increase for period: $147703.70
- Cash at the beginning of the period: $52,819.91
- Cash at the end of the period: $200,523.61

Chapter 9: Financial Must-Knows For Entrepreneurs

If you fully understood the previous chapter, then you are well-equipped to dive a little deeper in terms of financial numbers. In this chapter, I will be teaching you about important financial terminology. These are numbers that you absolutely need to know in order to run a successful business. I will also teach you how to properly understand them and help you analyze what the meaning of these numbers is. You will be learning about ROI, margins, break-evens, and fixed/variable costs. Don't worry; I will also teach you how to calculate each of these numbers. Let's get started.

Return On Investment (ROI)

Whether you are an investor or business owner, return on investment is an important analytical tool that you will need to use. The definition of ROI is the ratio of a profit/loss that is made in a fiscal year expressed in the terms of an investment. This number is always expressed as a percentage increase or decrease as it relates to the value of the investment during that fiscal year. Here is a simple example: if you invested $200 in stock, and its value rises to $220 at the end of that fiscal year, your return on investment is 10%. In a more complicated example, if you invested $1000 in coffee bean stock for your coffee business and at the end of the year, you generated $2200 from selling coffee made by the beans (assuming no other costs or taxes are involved), your ROI is 220%.

Here is the formula for ROI: Net Profit/Total Investment x 100% = ROI

Let's use this formula in a different example.

Imagine that you are in the business of flipping houses. You purchased a cheap house during a courthouse auction for $75,000 and then spent $35,000 in materials for renovations. After the sales of the house, commission, and expenses, you made $160,000 on the house. What would be your ROI?

First, you have to calculate your net profit which is your total revenue subtracted with your total costs. In this case, that would be $160,000 – ($75,000 + $35,000), this gives you $50,000. Remember, your costs are the purchase of the house ($75K) and the money you spend on materials ($35K).

Since ROI = Net Profit/Total Investment x 100
ROI = (50,000/110,000) x 100
ROI = 45 x 100
ROI = 45%

This may make house flipping sound easy but bear in mind that you can also lose money on an investment like this. If your investment is a loss, this formula will give you a negative number. Let's say, after everything, you could only sell the house for $90,000 as there are no other buyers. Take a look at the new ROI:

Revenue – Total Cost = Net Profit

$90,000 - $110,000 = -$20,000$

$ROI = Net Profit/Total Investment \times 100$

$ROI = (-20,000/110,000) \times 100$

$ROI = -0.182 \times 100$

$ROI = -18.2\%$

Essentially, you want your business to be yielding a positive number from your ROI; the higher, the better. If you are yielding a negative number, you may have to start rethinking your business plan or aiming to lower the cost of business.

Margins

In the world of finance, there are various different types of margins. The one that is most popularly used is the Profit Margin. There are also Operating Profit Margin, Net Profit Margin, and The Bottom Line. We will learn about all three of these in this chapter. Usually, a company's profit is calculated in three categories on its income statement. The most basic would be their gross profit and the most comprehensive being their net profit. In between these two exists the operating profit.

Gross Profit Margin

Let's start with the gross profit margin first. The gross profit margin is the profit of a business after accounting for the cost of goods sold (COGS). COGS includes the expenses that are DIRECTLY related to production and manufacturing, such as labor wages and raw materials. For instance, if you are a coffee bean seller, your COGS will be the cost of coffee beans purchased. Other figures are excluded in this figure, such as taxes, debt, overhead costs, operating costs, and large expenditures like the purchase of equipment. Here is the formula for the Gross Profit Margin:

Gross profit margin = (Net Sales − COGS)/Net Sales

Here is an example of gross profit margin: Imagine you are a café owner. You have spent $700 on goods such as; coffee beans, milk, and sugar. You also have one employee that you pay approximately $1200 per month. In this month, you have $2400 in revenue. What is your gross profit margin?

COGS = $700 + $1200
COGS = $1900

Gross profit margin = (Net Sales − COGS)/Net Sales
Gross profit margin = (2400 = 1900)/2400
Gross profit margin = 500/2400
Gross profit margin = 0.208
Gross profit margin = 20.8%

Operating Profit Margin

Operating profit margin is slightly more complex as it takes into account all other expenses such as; sales expenses, administrative expenses, operating expenses, and overhead expenses. These are all expenses that are necessary to keep the business running on a day-to-day business. This figure, however, still excludes non-operational expenses like debts and taxes. However, it DOES include the depreciation and amortization of assets. Here is the formula for operating profit margin:

Operating profit margin = (operating income/revenue) x 100

Let's use the same example above for this calculation. Here are the other expenses for your coffee shop: Rent is $300 per month, depreciation of your equipment such as coffee machines is $100 per month. Let's calculate your operating profit margin.

Revenue = $2400
COGS = $1900
Rent = $300
Depreciation = $100

Gross Profit = Revenue – COGS
Gross profit = 2400 – 1900
Gross profit = 500

Operating expenses = rent + depreciation
Operating expenses = 300 + 100
Operating expenses = 400

Operating income = Gross profit – Operating expenses
Operating income = 500 – 400
Operating income = 100

Operating profit margin = (operating income/revenue) x 100
Operating profit margin = (100/2400) x 100

Operating profit margin = 0.041 x 100
Operating profit margin = 4.1%

Net Profit Margin

So the net profit margin, otherwise known as the infamous "bottom line." This is the total amount of revenue that is left over after ALL expenses, and income types are accounted for. This will include the operational expenses we just talked about, COGS, and also other expenses such as taxes, debts, and any other payments. This number clearly reflects a business's ability to generate profit from their income. There are two formulas for this number:

Net profit margin = ((Revenue – COGS – Operating Expenses – Other expenses – Interest – Taxes)/Revenue) x 100

Net profit margin = (Net income/Revenue) x 100

Let's carry on with the coffee shop example we've used to calculate the net profit margin. Let's introduce other expenses that this coffee shop has. Imagine that this coffee shop needs to pay $250 in monthly taxes and $20 of monthly interest.

Taxes = $250
Interest = $20

Net profit margin = ((Revenue – COGS – Operating Expenses – Other expenses – Interest – Taxes)/Revenue) x 100

Net profit margin $= ((2400 - 1900 - 400 - 20 - 250)/2400)$ x 100

Net profit margin $= (-170/2400)$ x 100

Net profit margin $= -0.07$ x 100

Net profit margin $= -7\%$

As you can see through our series of calculations, at first glance, using the Gross profit margin, you would think that your coffee shop business is profitable. Even at the operating profit margin level, the business is still profitable. However, when you factor in ALL your expenses by calculating your net profit margin, aka your bottom line, your business is actually not profitable at all. By analyzing all three of these numbers, you are able to get an idea of whether your business is truly profitable or not.

Fixed/Variable Costs

Now, let's learn about fixed and variable costs. The two main costs that a company has are variable costs and fixed costs. The variable cost differs based on the amount that a business is producing while the fixed costs remain the same regardless of how much output the business is producing. Let's take a look at variable cost first.

Variable Cost

A company's variable cost is directly related to the amount of goods/services it is producing. This cost will decrease or increase based on the production volume. When business production increases, the variable cost will rise. If the business product decreases, then the variable cost will decline. Variable costs will differ widely between various industries. This means that it is not useful for you to compare the variable costs of a coffee shop to a car manufacturer because their product output is entirely different. It is much better to compare the variable costs between two companies within the same industry, such as another coffee shop.

Variable costs are calculated by multiplying the quantity of output by the variable cost per unit of output. For instance, let's say company A produces ceramic plates for $2 per plate. If this company produces 500 units, the variable cost will be $1000. However, if the company has no orders and therefore does not produce any plates, then the variable cost would be $0. If the company gets a large order of 10,000 plates, then the cost would rise to $20,000. Obviously, this calculation does not take into account other costs, such as raw materials or labor.

Fixed Cost

A fixed cost is the other cost that any business or company will have. Different from the variable cost, the fixed cost does not change based on the volume of production. It will remain consistent even if no goods/services are produced. This means that this cost cannot be avoided.

Let's use the same example for company A. Imagine that company A has a fixed cost of $10,000 per month for the rental of their plate producing machine. If the company has no orders for that month and doesn't produce any plates, they still have to pay $10,000 for the machine rental. However, let's imagine that they get a massive order of one million plates; the rental of that machine remains the same; $10,000. However, the variable cost will be $2M in this example.

The higher the fixed cost is for a company, the more revenue they will require in order to break even. This means that the company will need to sell more products and work harder because these costs usually are unable to be lowered. The most common fixed costs examples are; building leases/rent payments, certain salaries, interest payments, insurance, and utilities.

Variable costs tend to remain consistent based on the number of goods the company produces, but the effects of fixed costs on a company's bottom line can differ based on the number of goods it produces. When production goes up, fixed cost decreases. The price of a larger amount of goods can be spread out over the amount of a fixed cost. Due to this, a company can achieve economies of scale.

For instance, if company A has a $10,000 monthly lease on its factory and it produces 1000 plates per month. It can spread the fixed cost of the lease at $10 per plate. ($10,000/1000 plates) However, if company A produces 10,000 plates per month, then the fixed cost of its lease goes down to $1 per plate. W

Break-Even Analysis

The break-even analysis helps a business owner examine their margin of safety for their company based on their collected revenue and all costs. They can use this analysis to analyze different price levels and different demand levels. Essentially, the break-even analysis is used to determine what levels of sales are necessary to 100% cover the company's total fixed costs.

A break-even analysis is useful to determine the required level of production or the targeted desired sales mix. This analysis is normally used by management as these calculations and numbers aren't relevant to external people such as financial institutions, regulators, and investors. This analysis will depend on the calculation of the BEP (break-even point). The BEP is calculated by dividing the total fixed costs of production by the price of a product per individual unit minus the variable cost of production.

The break-even analysis will take a look at the number of fixed costs relative to the profit earned by each unit sold and produced. Usually, a company with lower fixed costs will have a lower BEP. For instance, if your company has $0 of fixed costs, you will break even automatically, and your first sale will generate a profit (considering that variable costs do not exceed your sales revenue).

The break-even analysis involves another financial figure, which is the contribution margin. The contribution margin is the difference between the selling price of a product and the total variable costs. So, let's say you are selling winter jackets for $100 each. The total fixed costs are $25 per unit for the sowing machine lease, and the total variable costs (cost of material) are $60 per jacket. The contribution margin of your jacket is $40 ($100 - $60). The remaining $40 is the amount of revenue that you will need to use to cover your remaining fixed costs, such as your $25 sowing machine lease and other costs like your rent or utilities.

The calculation of a break-even analysis can utilize two equations. The first equation divides the total fixed costs by the unit contribution margin. Let's use the example above of the jacket manufacturer. Let's say the total value of fixed costs if $20,000. If they have a contribution margin of $40, the BEP (break-even point) is 500 units (20,000/40 = 500). This means that when you are able to sell 500 jackets, the payment of your fixed costs is completed and the company will have a net profit/loss of $0.

You can use a different calculation for the BEP in sales dollars by dividing the total fixed costs by the contribution margin ratio. The contribution margin ratio is calculated by dividing the contribution margin per unit by the sale price. So if we use the same example, the contribution margin is 40% ($40 CM/$100 sale price/jacket = 40%). Therefore, the BEP in sales dollars is $50,000 ($20,000/40% = $50,000).

Chapter 10: Sales And Expenses 101

With your new knowledge of crucial financial figures like break-even analysis and fixed/variable costs, I can now teach you strategies to increase sales and reduce expenses. If you are finding that your company's BEP is too high or unattainable at the current business level that you have, reducing costs is a good option to lower than BEP. Let's learn about a few strategies.

How To Increase Sales

There are various different ways a business can try to increase their sales. We will be taking a look at distribution channels, sales mixes, and product selection.

Distribution Channels

The definition of distribution channels is quite simple. A distribution channel is the chain of businesses through which your goods/services will pass before it reaches the end consumer. Wholesalers, distributors, the internet, and retailers are different types of distribution channels. There are two types of questions you need to ask yourself to get an understanding of what your distribution channels are. "Who are my company's suppliers?" and "How do I get my product to the end buyer?"

Think about distribution channels like a map. This is the map of how your goods/services must travel in order for it to reach the end customer. On the other hand, it also describes how the consumer can make payments to get to the original vendor. Distribution channels can be very long or short; it highly depends on how many intermediaries are involved in delivering your service or product. Increasing the number of distribution channels so it's easier for a consumer to find your goods is a possible strategy to increase sales. However, having more intermediaries can make distribution management more expensive to manage. Having longer distribution channels could also cause you to earn less profit per item sold.

There are two types of distribution channels; direct and indirect. A direct channel is where the customer is able to buy goods from the manufacturer directly, while an indirect channel allows the customer to buy your goods from a retailer or wholesaler. Indirect channels are the traditional way that goods are sold in your brick and mortar retail store. For example, if you own a coffee shop business and a customer buys coffee beans from you, that is a direct-distribution channel. However, if your customer buys your beans at their local grocery shop and not at your store, that is an indirect channel.

There are three main types of distribution channels and they are all a combination of producer, wholesaler, retailer, and end customer. The first type of distribution channel is the longest as it includes the producer, wholesaler, retailer, and customer. The best example to describe this channel is the alcohol industry since there are many laws and regulations surrounding the selling and purchasing of alcohol. A typical winery is not allowed to sell their products directly to a retailer. Instead, they have to operate on a three-tier system, which means that the winery has to sell their products to a wholesaler first who then will sell the same product to a retailer. Then lastly, the retailer sells the same product to the customer.

The second type of distribution channel removes the wholesaler stage. This is where the producer sells their goods directly to a retailer who then sells the product to the customer. The total amount of intermediaries in this distribution channel is one. A good example of this is Dell. They are a large enough computer company that has the ability to sell their goods directly to large retailers such as Best Buy or Walmart.

The third type of distribution channel is the direct-to-consumer model, where the producer sells their products directly to the end customer. An example of this is a typical mom and pop shop like a bakery or a restaurant. They use their own store to sell directly to the end customer. This is the shortest type of distribution channel out there as it cuts out the retailer and the wholesaler.

Obviously, not all distribution channels will work for all products. As an entrepreneur, a strategic decision would be for you to choose the best distribution channel for your business. Your distribution channel strategy needs to align with your company's overall vision and mission statement. Your distribution method also needs to be strategic in a way that it can add value to the customer. Does your customer want to see the physical product before buying it? If your company offers services, would they want to speak to someone before purchasing? Or, do they simply just want to buy it online without any further communication? Finding the answers to these questions for your business will be important for you to choose the best distribution channel for your company.

Another area that you should consider is how quickly the customer would want the product to reach them. Specific products that have an expiry date like food and drinks may benefit the most with a direct distribution channel while other goods that don't expire may benefit the most with an indirect channel.

Sales Mix

The sales mix of a business is a calculation that determines how much of each product/service a business sells relative to the total sales. The sales mix is an important concept to understand and analyze as some services or products that a business offers can be more profitable than others. If a company changes its sales mix, its profits change as well. Managing your sales mix is a strategy and tool that business owners use to maximize company profits.

Many investors will utilize a company's sales mix to determine a company's prospects for profitability and overall growth. If they find that the company's profits are declining or flat, they may stop marketing or even stop selling a certain low-profit product and focus their efforts on selling their high-profit product.

As we learned in the earlier chapter, the profit margin is a company's net income divided by its total sales. This number is used to compare the profitability of two products that may be sold at different prices. Let's use an example. Let's say your coffee shop generates a net income of $15 on a coffee machine that sells for $300 and a net income of $2 on a bag of coffee beans that sells for $10. The profit margin on the bag of coffee beans is 20% ($2/$10 x 100%) and the coffee machine generates a profit margin of 5% ($15/$300 x 100%). This means that selling coffee beans is much more profitable than selling coffee machines, and as the café owner, you may want to shift your marketing efforts to promote your coffee beans as they bring you the highest profit margin.

The sales mix can also be used to help you strategize and plan business results to reach your target goals. For instance, let's say your coffee shop wants to earn $10,000 this month by generating $100,000 in total sales. You can then calculate different assumptions for your sales mix to determine a possible net income figure. If your coffee shop shifts the product mix towards the products with the highest profit margins, then the profit you make on every dollar sold will increase along with your net income. Another way to utilize your sales mix to strategize business results is by analyzing the inventory cost. For instance, if your coffee shop decided to stock more on the coffee machines to meet the Christmas demand, your coffee shop will earn lower profit margins than if it sold more bags of coffee. On top of that, stocking up on more coffee machines will require more physical space and large cash investment. There is also the expense of moving these large machines in and out of your store and your customers' home/vehicles. The more your coffee shop carries expensive products, the higher your inventory costs will be and will require you to invest large sums of cash.

Product Selection/Differentiation

Product selection or product differentiation is a marketing strategy that aims to distinguish your company's products or services from your competition's products or services. Successfully using product differentiation will require you to identify and communicate the unique qualities of your company's product/service offerings while emphasizing the differences between what you are offering and what other companies are offering. Your company's product differentiation works alongside your company's value proposition to make your products and services as attractive as possible to your audience or target market.

Product differentiations work to give your business a competitive advantage and to build brand awareness. For instance, the fastest high-speed internet (fiber optic) on the market right now is a differentiated product as few internet companies have this service.

The purpose of product differentiation is to convince the customer to choose your brand over a crowded industry of competitors. It is a set of qualities that set your product apart from other products that are similar. A common strategy that can be used for differentiation marketing is to focus your products and services on a niche market. For instance, a small company may find it hard to compete with larger competitors (e.g. local burger joint versus McDonald's). However, the smaller company may highlight a feature that their competitors don't have such as better customer service or money-back guarantee.

There are three main types of product differentiation; price, performance, and location. Price is something that can work both ways, you can choose to charge the lowest price possible to attract cost-conscious buyers. You could also charge a higher price to emphasize that your product/service is a luxury service and is worth it, such as a luxury car. Performance and reliability is another type of product differentiation. Traditionally, products that are considered reliable and could last a long-time is seen as better than other competitors. An example of this is a washing machine that is advertised to last for 20+ years may generate more sales than a washing machine that is advertised to last 5+ years only. Lastly, location can be a huge product differentiation, especially for smaller companies. These smaller companies usually market their brand as a local business and emphasize on their more personal service as a way for them to show customers that their business is worth the higher price.

How To Reduce Expenses

Now, let's take a look at a few strategies and tips that your company can use to reduce its expenses. There are only two ways that you could increase profits for your business; you could either increase your sales or reduce your expenses. Increasing sales is typically the harder route as it will involve a lot of strategies, planning, and moving pieces to pull off. However, reducing business expenses is something that is much easier to do and takes less time. Let's take a look at a few different ways that you can reduce business expenses to generate a larger bottom line.

1. Go digital

Printing costs are a huge expense that most companies don't realize can add up very quickly. The cost of ink, paper, and machine maintenance costs a small fortune, and a lot of time is wasted dealing with silly printing issues. As an entrepreneur, try to eliminate paper usage as much as possible to cut costs and streamline your business. Go digital as much as possible and take advantage of free software like Google drive and online signature services. This will also prevent problems like misplaced documents. Having everything digital will allow you and all of your employees to access important information quickly and cheaply.

2. Buy from big service providers

Big service providers typically have the lowest prices for materials you require, as they can operate on a lower profit margin. Smaller local options may seem better at first glance as they can customize their offerings to meet your needs. However, do some research on the big service providers first to see if they have any customizable offerings. This can help reduce your operating costs significantly.

3. Insurance

Depending on what your company offers, you may need to invest in some insurance. This could be liability insurance, building insurance, or car insurance. You need to regularly review your agreement with your insurance provider to figure out if another company can offer you a better deal. It doesn't take much time to do this and it can easily save you thousands of dollars every single year while your company is still receiving the same benefits. Some start-up insurance companies offer cheaper insurance premiums as they have lower costs by taking away office spaces and offering fully-remote work to their employees.

4. Hiring freelancers instead of staff when possible

Assess your company's needs when you feel like you require new talent to fix a business problem or to improve your business. If you require a website makeover, you don't need to hire a fulltime web developer to do this job. You can hire a freelancer easily to do the same job but without the long-term commitment. Outsource your work to contractors or freelancers whenever you can, but don't cheap out on them. Good contractors and freelancers typically cost a little bit more but it's much better to pay more upfront for high-quality work then to have to pay someone else to fix it later.

5. New equipment does not perform that much better than used equipment

Obviously, it is nice to buy new items but ensure that you are assessing the value of the new item you are buying in comparison to a similar secondhand item. For instance, if you are starting up your own coffee shop, look around your neighborhood buy and sell websites and forums to see if you can find the espresso machine model that you want but second hand. Most of the time, good equipment remains in good health even after many years, so buying a new espresso machine may not give you any additional benefits. Buying a second-hand machine may cost much less and provide you with the same services that you require.

6. Don't spend money on needless office space
If you are a business that does not regularly have clients coming and going, move your office space to somewhere less expensive or get rid of it altogether. With our convenient technology nowadays, you can even offer remote work for your employees to reduce the amount of physical space you need. If you require weekly meetings with your employees, rent a one-time space, or make it fun by having it at a local restaurant or bar.

Chapter 11: Financial Management

All businesses are faced with risks; a lot of these risks are actually due to improper financial management and decision making. The decisions that you make for your business can literally make or break it. Starting your business involves you to consider many things, this includes; what services/goods you are offering, your target market, resources required, and the investment you'd like to make. The question here is, how can you make better choices in all these aspects? Below are some pointers to help you avoid making bad financial decisions.

How To Avoid Making Bad Financial Decisions

Do research

The BEST thing you can do to avoid making bad financial decisions is to do your research. There is nothing that you can achieve without conducting the right research. Whether this is research for your target market or a specific product, it matters just as much. The bigger the decision you need to make, the more research is necessary. Make sure you are researching the potential risks of a business decision before jumping on it. While some risks are worth taking, other risks are not. Take notes and analyze the data that you've found to make the best decision for yourself.

Prioritize

IN a business, there are always three major aspects involved. The first aspect is your initial idea for your business. The second aspect is your investment. This is extremely important as your business is limited to how much funds are available to start it. The last investment is time. By optimizing all three aspects, you can ensure that your business is productive. Prioritizing the tasks and ideas required to bring out the best of your business is key. For instance, don't focus on generating more investment if you don't have a solid business idea. Prioritize your tasks in an order that makes sense to ensure that you are not wasting time on tasks that don't need to be completed yet.

Choose the right investment

Not every investment that you make will produce large results. This is because not every investment is the right one. Sometimes, entrepreneurs make bad investments in areas that their company does not benefit from. You need to be asking yourself whether or not your next investment is going to provide you with substantial results. If not, you shouldn't spend that money. An area that a lot of companies mistakenly spend their money on is marketing. Before you spend big bucks on a marketing plan, analyze how well your business is doing first. If it's not doing well at all, this may not be a marketing error and it may be a matter of lack of demand for your product/service. If you are getting some business but not all of it, then investing in marketing may be necessary to gain more market share.

Don't shy away from making hard decisions

Although this may sound like common sense, the root of bad business decisions is usually due to a person's inability to make tough decisions. Often times as business owners and entrepreneurs, we are faced with hard choices that require an immediate decision. Running a business means that you need to be firm with your decisions. This could range from firing someone who is dragging down your business or breaking free from a partnership. This could even mean giving up on a particular service/product and rethink your business plan entirely.

Do not delay debt payments

Debt and loans are common aspects of all businesses. There isn't any harm in taking out a loan to invest in your business, but the problem begins if you are unable to repay your debts on time. The more you delay paying off debt, the worse it gets. The interest that will be charged due to late payments is one of the biggest enemies for a business. This can decrease the credit score of your business and financial status. Ensure that when you are taking out a loan, you are sure that you will be able to repay every payment on time. If you are unsure about this, it may not be the right decision for your business at the time. For instance, let's say you are thinking of purchasing a $10,000 marketing plan with installments of $1,000 every month for your consulting business. How sure are you that you will be able to pay back the $1,000 every month even if your business doesn't grow? Is your business making enough money right now to cover that $1,000 if the marketing plan fails? Analyze your own business and ask yourself objective questions. Don't take out any loans if you aren't confident that you will be able to pay it back without delay.

Choosing Different Accounting Methods To Produce Desired Results

Believe it or not, most people don't give their accounting much thought for their small businesses. You may have an accountant that just does your taxes for you without even asking you if you have any preferences. There are actually two main accounting methods for small businesses; cash vs. accrual basis accounting.

As the business owner, you need to know the difference between these two types of accounting and understand which you are eligible to use and when each method is the best choice for you. With small business taxes, cash basis, or accrual basis accounting can have huge consequences on you. Keep in mind that different countries have different tax regulations, so please consult your accountant on these differences. For example purposes, we will be using U.S. regulations for our examples.

Typically, the IRS will require all businesses to use a consistent and standardized accounting method each year for business taxing. If you decide to use a different accounting method down the line, you have to get approval from the IRS. The IRS will allow businesses to choose from accrual basis, cash basis, a specialized method, or a hybrid method to report your taxes. If you don't use the same accounting method consistently, you are at risk of IRS not accepting your return, and you may be required to pay fines or additional taxes. Let's learn about the functions of cash and accrual methods.

Cash Basis Accounting

Cash basis is the most common method that small businesses use for their accounting. In cash basis accounting, the income that you make is recorded when it's received. For instance, let's say you own a consulting company, and you did work for a client on May 20th. You then created an invoice with a due date of June 1st. You will record the income for your work when the customer pays you in June instead of May when you actually delivered the work. The premise of cash basis accounting is that your income is recorded when you receive your payment from the customer, not when you have delivered the work or billed the customer. Similarly, your expenses are recorded when you have paid them, not when you have ordered them. Let's say you forgot to pay your office rent in June. When you receive your rent bill in July, you notice that you are billed twice the amount. After you verify that you did indeed not pay the rent for June, you will need to write a check to pay both month's rent by July 1st. You will then record this full payment amount as an expense in July which means that no rent payment will be recorded in your financial statements for the month of June.

There are many benefits to cash-based accounting, the main one being that record keeping is easy. If you are recording your income as you receive it and expenses as you pay them, you can literally do all your accounting work without needing to hire an external accountant. If you use this method, you don't need to enter bills and invoices into any business/accounting software. However, these functions are still useful as you can then ensure that no expenses or income are being missed. Another benefit to cash basis accounting is that it helps you track your cash flow. Having this analysis handy will allow you to get a good idea of what your business' cash flow is like and how it's changing.

However, there are some downsides to this accounting method. Cash basis can easily give you an unrealistic picture of how your business is doing. Let's look back at the example where you billed your customer in May, but your customer actually paid their invoice in June. Let's say that you did a ton of work at the end of May, but none of your customers paid until June. When you look back on these statements in the future, you may think that May was a very busy month, and June was slow because of the amount of money you received in June. From this information, you may decide to make business decisions such as reducing labor costs in May or even taking some time off then. This can be a huge mistake for your business as the truth is that you were busy in May, not in June. You had simply just received payment for your work in May, in June. Some other downsides to cash basis accounting include difficulty tracking profitability monthly and the need to track accounts payable and receivable separately.

Profitability is hard to track per month as sometimes your invoices and expenses aren't paid in the same month, although they were meant for that same month. Let's think back to that example where you forgot to pay rent in June and had to pay double rent in July. Since a double rent payment was paid for in July, it can skew your expenses dramatically and make June look like a more profitable month than July when in reality, business could've been the same or slightly worse in June.

Accrual Basis Accounting

Accrual basis accounting is more commonly used by larger companies but smaller ones can benefit from it too. In accrual basis accounting, your business income is recorded when it's earned (opposite from cash basis). Back to the example we used, the work that you've done in May would show up on May's financial statement and not June's. Similarly, expenses are also recorded when it's incurred, not when you pay it. In our missed rent payment scenario, although you forgot to pay June's rent and had to pay it in July, your financial statements would show a rent expense in June.

There are many benefits to accrual basis accounting. The first benefit is that it tracks your business performance much better than cash basis accounting. Accrual basis accounting allows you to easily see when your business is most or least profitable on a monthly basis. Based on your financial statements, you may be able to make accurate business decisions like increasing your workforce during May to accommodate more customers rather than cutting your labor down. Accrual basis accounting helps business owners forecast and budget better. Secondly, accrual basis accounting gives the business owner better abilities to track monthly profits. You can see your true net profit for each month, which helps to prevent the common mistake of overcommitting on expenses. Lastly, accrual basis accounting is typically what investors and lenders prefer. These people want to have a clear view of how your company's doing, and accrual basis accounting is the best way to see this picture clearly.

There are some downsides to this accounting method. Firstly, it makes it harder to detect any cash flow issues. In accrual basis accounting, there is a third financial statement that is critical to your business decisions. Let's go back to that example where you delivered work in May but got paid in June. Your net profit in the month of May is going to look great. However, your bank account may be sitting at $0 because you haven't actually been paid yet. This means that you will want to analyze your profit and loss statements side by side with your cash flow statement to ensure you are actually being paid. Secondly, this accounting method requires more time and labor to administer. When you are running your financial reports, you have to make sure all your bills for expenses and invoices to the customer have been inputted into your system before you can produce reports. This may make the end of the month stressful, especially if you aren't inputting this information as you go. Hiring a professional accountant in this scenario would be immensely helpful. Lastly, accrual basis accounting can lead to you paying higher taxes. This is because you are recording your income exactly on the date that you earned it which means that you could be paying taxes on income that haven't actually reached your bank account yet.

Which Accounting Method Should You Choose?

For simplicity's sake, most small business owners will choose cash basis accounting. However, we can't deny the benefits that come with accrual basis accounting if you want to get a realistic read on how your business is doing.

Cash basis accounting is the best method for the following situations:

1. You are just starting your business and you are a sole proprietor

Cash basis accounting doesn't require as much learning, and studying as accrual-basis accounting does. This is the best method for those that are low on cash and have just started their business that is likely juggling many responsibilities at one time. If you can't afford an accountant or don't have the need for it yet, this method is the simplest way to keep track of your finances.

2. You are a business with low investment, and you're preparing for tax season

If your business is new with not that much income coming in yet and you are worried about paying your taxes, cash basis accounting is useful for you as it shows you exactly how much cash you have on hand. For instance, if you had serviced a client before the tax filing deadline but your client hasn't paid their invoice yet, then you can report that sale for next year's taxes.

Accrual accounting is the best method for the following situations:

1. Your business has an average gross revenue of $25M+ across a three-year period

The IRS is flexible regarding which accounting method you want to use but if your business averages over $25M, then you have to file your taxes via accrual basis. Any less than that, then you are able to choose whichever accounting method you like.

2. Your business has inventory

Businesses that have inventory were required to utilize accrual basis accounting according to previous law. However, due to recent tax changes, as long as your business has under $25M of revenue in the last three years, you can treat your inventory as non-incidental materials or choose an accounting method that is best for your business.

3. You have to file sales tax

Certain states (like New York) require business owners to file sales taxes on an accrual basis. Be sure to do research in the state that you reside, or else you may find yourself needing to pay sales tax on an invoice that you haven't had payment for yet. This could have terrible effects on your cash flow. In this situation, an accountant would be in your best interest to help you figure out whether or not this applies to your business.

Chapter 12: Additional Tips And Tricks To Help You Become A Successful Entrepreneur

With your new knowledge of the proper mindset and financial understanding, we can take your financial intelligence and entrepreneurship to the next level by learning about more tips. It doesn't matter if you are someone who is starting their first business or if you are well into your 20th business – you still want to be successful. The ability to own your own business gives people a strong sense of empowerment. You are responsible for making all of your decisions, taking your vision, and making it real and building life-long relationships with customers and other people. Here are thirty more tips related to entrepreneurship for your consumption:

1.   Get gritty and PERSEVERE

One of the first things you learned about in this book is building a habit of perseverance. Grit is perseverance. Entrepreneurs NEED to have a go-getter attitude, which is the ability to keep working despite all the obstacles and people telling you that you should give up your dream. Successful entrepreneurs are some of the grittiest people in the world. So get gritty.

2.   Challenge yourself in every way possible

As I said, you have to hold your self accountable as an entrepreneur. If you want to be successful, you have to keep challenging yourself to reach more goals – no one is going to tell you to do these things. In fact, challenges should keep you on your toes. If you are someone who is always excited for a challenge, keep yourself on your toes and accept all challenges that come your way.

3. Be passionate about your business

As an entrepreneur, you need to love what you do, or else you will struggle more with things like procrastination and motivation. The nature of building your own business from scratch requires you to put in long and hard hours, if you aren't willing to make sacrifices in your life to accommodate that, this may not be from you. To build a business of something you are passionate about. Do something you love, so you don't get tired of it.

4. Take calculated risks

Naturally, people are risk-averse. People don't usually like to take risks unless they have to. However, a part of being an entrepreneur has the ability to take the risks that work for you. It's a part of the job. The most successful entrepreneurs in the world understand which risks they should take and which they should stay away from. Get yourself used to risks and begin to learn the ones that will benefit your business and the ones that won't. If you take a risk and fail, it's okay – that's all a part of the obstacles that come with entrepreneurship. Learn from your lesson and try again.

5. Trust yourself

As an entrepreneur, you are going to have a lot of people doubting you and telling you that you're wasting yourself. People aren't just going to automatically give their trust to you, so if you don't trust yourself, nobody else will. Listen to your intuition and rely on your knowledge and wisdom when making business decisions. Be confident and show people that you trust yourself as people are more likely to follow a leader who is confident. With that said, there is also nothing wrong with asking for help when you need it. Having a mentor is a great idea, and you shouldn't feel ashamed to reach out to one for advice. Learn to trust yourself, and you are already in a great position to be successful.

6. Reduce fear of failure

Actions are stopped due to fear. As an entrepreneur, you have to be able to overcome feelings of fear and take action quickly when you identify an opportunity or if you're bouncing back from a mistake. If you are constantly afraid of everything you are faced with, you won't be a successful entrepreneur. Don't ignore your fear completely, as that can cause big mistakes to happen but use fear as your guide instead. Use it to judge the risks you are planning to take but don't let it completely cloud you at the same time. The more you get yourself accustomed to making certain decisions, the less fear you will fear, and the clearer you will be able to think.

7. Visualize your goals

We learned in the earlier chapters that visualization is a great tool for you to learn and master new skills.

Visualizing your goals will also help you seem them in a more tangible and real way. Make sure you are not only visualizing your end goal, visualize each and every step that will take you there also. The more accustomed you get to your plan, the easier it will feel in its execution.

8. Hire great partners

Hiring strong partners may seem obvious, but the reality is everybody needs a little bit of help when accomplishing their dream. Hire people that not only have good hard skills in the business you're in but someone with good character that you can respect. In fact, if it comes down to choosing between strong hard skills and good character – always choose a good character. You can always teach skills, but you can't teach a person morals and ethics.

9. Act, don't react

Successful entrepreneurs don't sit around, waiting for the right opportunity to come along; they simply just act. It's easy to get caught up in all the things you need to think about, like funding or predicting potential failures but just talking about these things won't do anything. Take action to mitigate risk and build a plan.

10. Spend time

There is no such thing as an overnight success, and no entrepreneur has found success in just one night. You may not see any results in your first week, month, or even year. This is normal. Successful entrepreneurs have put in thousands of hours with no result until finally, there is. Keep putting in the hours and keep adapting; before you know it you'll become successful.

11. Plan your finances
We all know that every business starting up requires money – that's just how it works. One of the biggest mistakes that entrepreneurs make is spending too much of their time looking for investors and not enough time focusing on other areas of their business. Make a plan for your finances but be sure that you are completing other required business tasks at the same time.

12. Identify your customer
The main reason for failing start-ups is that there isn't a customer. If you are starting a business without a known customer base, the case may be that the customer doesn't actually exist. Before you start your business altogether, do research, and find out if there is a customer base for the product/service you are selling. Then, build your business around this information.

13. Take complaints as feedback
One tip that entrepreneurs need to learn is that you need to listen to your customer's complaints. This is pretty much free business advice. Don't get defensive, but take a look at their reviews objectively. This will not only help you identify areas in your business that needs improvement, but you will also gain the respect of the customer by acknowledging their complaint.

14. Exceed customer expectations

Always ensure that your business is not just meeting expectations, exceed expectations every single time. If you are able to deliver more than what your customers expect, you will be guaranteed referrals and loyal customers.

15. Manage your risks

Remember when we talked about risk earlier? We should always take risks when running your business, but you shouldn't be taking on every single risk that presents itself. Instead, manage your risks by learning to walk away from those that aren't worth taking.

16. Read case studies

As an entrepreneur, you may be tempted to use your time-off and evenings to consume entertainment, like watching television or movies. Instead of watching a new Netflix original series, I encourage you to read case studies related to entrepreneurship. The more you know, the more educated you will be when you are faced with the next business decision.

17. Self-promote

Many people have a fear of self-promoting as they don't want to come off as an egomaniac. However, if you aren't going to promote your business, nobody else will. Build a 15-second elevator pitch for yourself, so you are ready to go when someone asks you about your business. You can then walk them through it quickly and factually.

18. Define company culture

In our modern-day, company culture is extremely important. With the glaring eyes of the media, companies strive to be better than ever before. Set a positive culture for your company starting from day one, and you'll attract higher quality employees, partners, and even customers.

19. Network as much as you can

Networking is a good idea for every working individual but it is even better for entrepreneurs. Never stop networking, get out there, and meet people as you never know what you might find. Even if the people you find aren't able to directly help your business, you may be able to meet someone that can offer invaluable insight to you.

20. Learn and create

A successful entrepreneur is a person that has a mindset that is willing to learn and to create new things. The important part of building your own business is your ability to learn new things and execute them. Like we learned earlier in this book, spend time learning new skills that are beneficial to your business. Use your spare time to hone your skills rather than binging a new TV show.

21. Deliver, don't sell

Everybody knows that nobody likes to be sold to. Rather than selling your product/service to your customers, deliver them instead. Offer some sort of free trial that gives them a taste of your product. Then, whatever you are offering will sell itself.

22. Take baby steps

Thinking about the largeness of your goal can be very daunting, that's normal and totally okay. Starting a business from nothing is a huge task. Like we talked about throughout this book, the fool-proof tactic is to break it down into smaller steps and goals. Once you have smaller steps, crossing them off one at a time will help you make progress.

23. Put everything on your calendar

Put EVERYTHING into your calendar. Whether it's conference calls, meetings, or even happy hour with your team – put it in. Once things are in your calendar, there are no excuses for why you can't do it, you have made the time for it. Schedule in things like exercise, your afternoon snack, and even a 15-minute break – this will help you break up your day to keep you sharp for other tasks.

24. Exercise frequently

We learned earlier in this book that exercise is one of the healthiest habits you can implement in your life. Just because you want to be a successful entrepreneur does not mean you don't have time to work on your physical health. As I mentioned above, book time to go to the gym, go for a run, or even just go for a stroll in your neighborhood. Stay physically active at least once a day helps you take care of your mind and body.

25. Focus

The daily tasks of an entrepreneur can feel disjointed and scattered, which is why it is important to limit the time spent on multitasking. Lots of scientific research has shown that multitasking is not beneficial and humans are not meant for it. Try to focus on just doing one task at a time. Giving one task 100% of your attention and focus will actually help you get it done faster and in a higher quality.

26. Take time off

The toughest thing for an entrepreneur to put into practice is taking time off. Many people in North America don't do this often enough. Although you may not need frequent time off, you do need to take some time off. This doesn't have to be a full-blown tropical vacation, make time for a 2 – 3-day break where you can just rest your mind and body in your own home.

27. Ask questions

Nobody knows everything. Always ask for help and seek advice from your fellow entrepreneurs or mentors, you know. Asking questions will help you learn more about your task at hand. Don't be shy.

28. Failing is learning

I have mentioned numerous times throughout this book that failure is inevitable. You will fail and you will need to accept it. Get used to it, and don't let it faze you. Pick yourself back up and keep at it.

29. Get inspired

As an entrepreneur, you need to get creative to solve problems and make new connections. To do this, you need to have a source of inspiration. Make time for things that inspire you, whether it's chatting with your mentor, reading a new book, or building something.

30. Help others

Entrepreneurs are very busy people, so it is easy to think that you don't have time to help others.

However, helping people actually ignites inspiration and is extremely beneficial. It feels good to help other people, so find an opportunity to help someone out and you never know what might come out of it in the future.

Chapter 13: Welcome Your Failures

An important concept I want you to understand is that failure is welcome when you are striving towards a goal. Do not begin your journey of entrepreneurship thinking that you aren't going to fail. That is only going to discourage you from picking yourself back up. There will be days where you stay in bed instead of going to a networking event, or you decide to binge-watch another Netflix original rather than putting in hours into your business. Having failures is completely okay as long as you learn from it and find a way to overcome it next time around. The best way to overcome failure is to prevent it in the first place. If you are going to have drinks with friends, buy a case of beer and invite them over – that way, you have to stop drinking as you will run out of beer. If you are planning to go to the gym in the morning, call your workout buddy and ask them to come with you to the gym. That way, you won't want to stand them up so you'll be forced to go. Preventing these failures will keep you from moving forward. However, some failures may be unavoidable, and that's okay too. Use your self-discipline to pick yourself back up whenever a failure knocks you down.

What Is The Edison Mentality?

This is where the 'Edison Mentality' comes in. Thomas Edison truly believes that his success was inevitable. He made sure to align all his goals with what his passions were. This created a powerful sense of motivation and optimism that has a positive effect on everyone around him. This included his family, friends, customers, coworkers, investors, and ultimately, the entire nation. He didn't give up the first time he failed on his journey. He created innovative ways to overcome the obstacles he was faced with. He wasn't disappointed when he faced a problem that halted his progress. He embraced it with open arms because he EXPECTED it. Expect yourself to fail, but create a plan that will help you overcome it. That is how you can use failure to teach yourself more self-discipline.

In fact, permanent failure is usually caused by low self-discipline. That is the failure you don't want. You want to encounter failures that motivate you to grow and increase your self-control and innovative thinking. If you have low self-discipline, even if you promised your workout buddy to meet you at the gym in the morning, you still won't go because you don't value your commitment to the gym and not to your friend.

Disciplined People Are Unfazed By Failure

By having strong self-discipline and a positive mindset, you can also be unfazed by failure. Do you know why disciplined people are unfazed by failure? It's because they don't care about what knocked them down; they only care about getting back up and achieving their goal. As an entrepreneur, you will experience a variety of failures. Don't let one failure define your business. Don't let one failure be the cause of its demise. Pick yourself back up and think about what you can do to prevent this failure in the future or what you can do to overcome it. The people that give up on their entrepreneurship are usually those with low self-discipline. Let's take a look at some causes of low self-discipline. This will help you avoid some of these causes.

Causes Of Low Self-Discipline

High self-discipline helps people establish their inner strength and character, enables them to withstand temptation, increases their chance of success, builds better relationships, and has more resistance to feeling offended. We will now discuss some of the causes as to why some people have low self-discipline. Having low self-discipline, not unlike having high self-discipline, affects people's performance in multiple aspects of their life. This includes the performance at work, school, relationships, sports, and financial well-being.

Lack of self-discipline shows up in all the different things that people do in their lives. Some people make sure that they do the big things in life but end up neglecting the little things. They do this to impress other people who don't know them very well. However, they tend to annoy and disappoint those that are close to them because it shows that they don't care enough about the people that they should be showing respect to.

One of the reasons why people don't take more responsibility for everyday obligations is because they don't believe in its importance. Why is this? Why do some people take the time to be considerate, clean, trustworthy, and honest, while others believe that those things are important? The answer is their attitude towards themselves, other people, and life itself. The former believe that people, including themselves, and other forms of life are worth investing their energy, time, resources, and interest into.

They are able to see the importance of life while the latter have less regard for life and for themselves. All of the simply relates to love. When people have a love for life, they tend to respect all components of it. They take the time to appreciate and experience life as if it's a pleasure. Self-discipline comes from the willingness to take care of ourselves, other people, and other types of life. The lack of discipline shows less willingness to respect themselves or other things.

The second reason why people don't take more responsibility for everyday obligations is because of the lack of commitment. A person's commitment, enthusiasm, and interest to a task determine the degree to which they can be distracted. When their commitment is very high, very few things have the power to distract them, but if they are doing something that is meaningless to them, their attention is easily distracted.

This proves a strong link between self-discipline and commitment. People who have the inability to ignore, control, or bypass thoughts means that they have low self-discipline.

By learning the reasons behind why a person does not take more responsibility for everyday obligations, we are ready to learn the six causes of poor self-discipline.

Cause #1: Low self-awareness

The primary cause of low self-discipline is a lack of awareness. This component is important specifically to our imagination and thinking. People are unaware of the thoughts that take our attention are actually negative and can damage a person's well-being.

These thoughts are fed into the conscious mind by the negative mind power to ensure that people have minimal time to spend just simply just being mindful. If people are aware of the things that are happening within their own minds, they would know that self-discipline is needed to refocus our attention away from the flow of negative thoughts.

Cause #2: General character weaknesses

People who have weak character often creates poor self-discipline. This includes aspects that have a low level of inner strength, mental toughness, courage, lack of love for other people, an absence of self-love, low interest in self-improvement, apathy, and a version of hard work, shortage of responsibility. Lack of self-reflection, high levels of greed, and the inability to ignore temptations in general.

If people place more importance on the desires, thoughts, and emotions that harm them more than the actions, thoughts, and people that help them, it will be difficult for them to develop high self-discipline. Each moment comes with a choice that a person has to make. It can either be something that helps them reach the goals they have set for themselves, or they can fall into temptation and choose the action that has instant gratification.

Cause #3: Low ambition

Ambition is very effective in creating self-discipline by giving us a reason to work towards our goals, although we might rather be doing something else. However, it has a negative effect on our self-discipline if our ambition is in an honorable, ethical, or fulfilling one. It is obvious that people who lack the ambition to achieve goals in life will have a harder time building strong self-discipline because they don't have a reason to do it.

This is why we discussed in chapter one that one of the main steps in developing strong self-discipline is coming up with clear and attainable goals. By coming up with a goal that is realistic, an individual can then create a plan of action that they can then hold themselves accountable to. They also need to continue finding the motivation and ambition to keep them striving towards their goals.

Cause #4: Low importance goals

People that have goals that aren't that important tend to lack the ambition to achieve them and, therefore, will not be able to practice their self-discipline. If people set goals that looked good on the outside but didn't actually believe that they were necessary, or didn't see them as goals that are important enough to accomplish in the first place, then they may find it very difficult exercise self-discipline in order to put in the work to achieve them.

One of the main motivating factors of self-discipline is having a goal that a person is able to stand by or is important to them. By having an important goal, or something that is meaningful to them, they will be able to find the self-discipline needed in order to complete the tasks required in order to achieve their goal.

Cause #5: Laziness

There are many temporary reasons as to why a person is not exhibiting self-discipline to do the things that need to be done. This could be sickness, tiredness, apathy, or something that is more appealing that is immediately available. If you find that these excuses are often occurring when you were trying to complete the task needed to reach a goal, you need to dig deep and find the real reason why you are choosing options that aren't the ones that will help you achieve your goal.

Laziness is often the culprit in a lot of cases. The reasons for laziness usually runs very deep into an individual's psyche. If a person believes that there is a goal that is worthwhile, they will be motivated to keep working and applying themselves and making the decisions that make sense when it comes to achieving their goal. However, if they don't have any motivation to achieve their goal, it likely means that their goal isn't important enough, or the person has a natural tendency to be lazy and uninterested.

Cause #6: Lack of self-respect

A person who is lacking self-respect often doesn't put a lot of effort or importance in achieving personal excellence. They often don't really care what others think about them or whether or not they are helping out other people in their lives. You might be wondering what self-respect has to do with self-discipline. The answer is that it takes self-discipline in order to produce excellent results, to achieve goals, and to help people who require it. When a person doesn't think about their own self-improvement, they tend to focus on other things that bring them pleasure such as instant gratification.

They don't necessarily practice self-discipline because they are comfortable in indulging the instant gratification that life throws at them. If a person lacks respect for themselves, they are more likely to indulge in unhealthy conveniences like fast food or shopping impulses that we discussed in chapter one. If a person does have self-respect for themselves, they understand that this instant gratification may bring them joy and pleasure at the moment, but does very little in helping them achieve healthy long-term goals.

By understanding the psychology behind the concept of self-discipline, willpower, and self-control, a person is more likely to see the importance of having these traits if they are a person that wants to achieve the goals they have in life. I strongly believe that everyone has their own personal goals that they want to accomplish in their life. Those who say they don't may simply be too afraid of failure, and hide their fear behind their lies about how they don't have goals rather than coming to terms with the fact that they are scared of failing to achieve their goals.

Conclusion

Congratulations on reaching the end of this book! There has been a lot of new information taught to you that you probably need some time to digest. The main takeaway that I wanted to emphasize before we finish off is that your mindset and discipline are JUST as important as your financial literacy. You can always get ramped up on financial knowledge or even hire a person to take care of that for you, but what you cannot do is learn mindset and discipline without putting in the work. Ensuring that you start your journey or entrepreneurship on the right foot is crucial.

The first thing you should work on before anything else is your self-discipline. With strong self-discipline, you can utilize this skill to do any other task or learning that you require. Self-discipline requires the use of your willpower and habits. By building all the right habits that help you complete tasks when they need to be done will ensure that you are maximizing your productivity. Remember to break down all your large goals and tasks into smaller and more digestible pieces. We learned that procrastination is an entrepreneur's greatest enemy, and procrastination usually appears when we are faced with an overwhelming task. By breaking every large task down to manageable pieces, we are ensuring that our habits and self-discipline will take on from there and you can complete required tasks before their deadline, always.

Once you have accomplished your business enough, and you have started makings sales and have incurred your expenses, this would be a great time to build upon your financial literacy. In this book, you have learned the basics of finance and various strategies you can use to maximize your business profitability. Take this one step further, learn more, and keep yourself discipline and NEVER take on more debt than you think you can manage. As you are furthering your skills and knowledge in the world of finance and entrepreneurship, never forget to keep a healthy mindset and strong self-discipline. With a combination of financial literacy, mindset, and self-discipline, you are well on your way to running a successful business.

Remember, every entrepreneur has been faced with failure. You will be no different. Be sure that you are not giving up if you have failed and that you are always making plan B and plan C to overcome potential obstacles. Take every failure as a learning lesson, so it doesn't happen again. As long as you are willing to pick yourself up from any failure, there is no reason why you won't become a successful entrepreneur. Figure out what strategies and methods are best with your business and stick with them until you feel like a change needs to happen. Keep yourself updated on your market and industry. Look out for existing competition and new competition. Be dynamic, and don't get stuck on your old ways but also don't flip flop your strategy too much. Write your results down and analyze the work you've done and what other competitors have done. Knowledge is key here, having the discipline and mindset to stay on top of your business and your industry will be your secret recipe to outlasting and beating all your competitors. I wish you the best of luck on your journey and remember, keep a strong mindset and stay disciplined.

****

CPSIA information can be obtained
at www.ICGtesting.com
Printed in the USA
FSHW021257011121
85891FS

9 781777 330408